W9-CBP-944

THE UNTOUCHABLES
THREE GENERATIONS OF
TRIUMPH OVER TORMENT

Solomon Darwin

Peaceful Evolution Publishing

WITHDRAWN FROM
RAPIDES PARISH LIBRARY
Alexandria, Louisiana
RB

THE UNTOUCHABLES

THREE GENERATIONS OF
TRIUMPH OVER TORMENT

Stories of Empowerment through
Faith, Entrepreneurship,
Education and Equal Opportunity

Solomon Darwin

Peaceful Evolution Publishing

© 2018 Peaceful Evolution Publishing
All rights reserved.

No part of this publication may be reproduced, distributed, or transmitted in any form or by any means, including photocopying, recording, or other electronic or mechanical methods, without the prior written permission of the publisher, except in the case of brief quotations embodied in critical reviews and certain other noncommercial uses permitted by copyright law.

ISBN-13: 9781981064564
ISBN-10: 1981064567

Printed in the United States of America.

Peaceful Evolution Publishing
Suite 402J
220 Piedmont Avenue
Berkeley, CA 94720

Contact: peacefulevolutionpublishing.com

First Edition
14 13 12 11 10 / 10 9 8 7 6 5 4 3 2 1

Editor: Jon Zilber
Associate Editor: Sue Fry
Cover Design: Dan Quita
Book Layout & Design: David Grebow

TABLE OF CONTENTS

WHEN THE UNTHINKABLE AND IMPOSSIBLE BECOMES INEVITABLE

Some things that may seem impossible are not only possible, they're inevitable. This is the story of three members of India's Untouchable caste—my grandmother, my father, and myself—doing many things that should have been impossible. But sometimes doing the impossible is part of your destiny.

I was born an Untouchable in a village in India. In traditional Indian culture, all people are born into one of several castes, ranked from highest (Brahmins) to lowest (Untouchables). The life of an Untouchable consists primarily of doing work that is considered to be beneath the people of other castes. Other castes view Untouchables as less-than-human creatures, who share drinking water with animals and are suited only for undesirable tasks, such as dealing with human waste and dead bodies.

I speak of the lives of Untouchables in the present tense. While the caste system is no longer legally recognized, its social and cultural legacy is still very much a reality, especially in the small villages where 70% of Indian people live. Just as the end of Apartheid in South Africa or civil rights legislation in America may have changed the official stance on racial segregation or discrimination, laws can't immediately heal racial divisions or instantly end patterns of segregation that have been reinforced for many generations.

In India, the caste system has existed for over 3,500 years.

The heritage and legacy of the caste system remains a powerful force in India, one still lodged deeply in the hearts of many people. In cities, the caste system is less prominent than in the more remote villages of India, but even there it remains a deeply rooted part of society. Marriages between two people of different castes, for example, certainly raises eyebrows—and often prompts overt hostility. Some have noted that the present-day caste system is still the largest manifestation of discrimination on the planet, affecting roughly 150 million people.

The caste system is also often misunderstood outside of India. Many Westerners are familiar with the ideas of karma and reincarnation and may find them to be alluring concepts. But in Indian culture, these ideas don't exist in a vacuum. They are pillars that form the foundation for the caste system; the parameters of your current life are driven by your actions in a previous life. The caste system is a consequence of these concepts.

In Indian culture, your caste is your birthright—or for some, your "birthwrong"—that is based on the karmic balance sheet of your actions in your previous life. Being born an Untouchable is often considered to be a just outcome for your behavior in previous lives; it is a fair punishment for the crimes you may not remember committing but can't deny. Or, perhaps in your next life, you'll be rewarded by being born into a higher caste, moving up the caste ladder one life at a time.

Not only are Untouchables expected to spend their days doing demeaning work, they all live in a segregated world, shunned by most other Indians. Members of my caste are born into families with house names that reflect their lowly stature—these family names translate into Indian words for parasites and scavenger animals, such as "worm" or "leech." Even at birth, our names clearly and instantly telegraph — to ourselves and others — that we are to live as scavengers.

As the name Untouchables makes clear, members of our caste are not to be touched by members of other castes. Historically, Untouchables lived in mud huts in their own villages; whenever an Untouchable stepped on the land, entered a building, or sat in a chair used by other castes, the higher castes felt their property had been contaminated or violated. Facilities for Untouchables — such as schools or medical centers — are few and far between, and often their services are little more than a charade.

Untouchables have sometimes been subjected to horrific situations that would be unimaginable for most people. In so-called "swinging ceremonies," for example, an Untouchable would swing from a metal hook in excruciating pain; their agony supposedly serving as a proxy to "purify" the member of a higher caste holding the ceremony. While some of the worst atrocities of the caste system may no longer exist, Untouchables still endure extremely harsh lives. And while it may be hard for Westerners to understand, many Untouchables accept their lot in life.

It is my belief, however, that the caste system arose as a result of the selfish and base nature of humanity, not as a result of any specific Hindu doctrine. Charity and the idea of dharma, or the cosmic order of things, are key pillars of Hinduism, the prevailing Indian faith; it is clear that the harsh and cruel consequences of the caste system do not derive from Hindu teachings. Indeed, most cultures have developed their own version of a caste system, despite having very different religious, social, and economic traditions. European feudalism, American slavery, and the treatment of women in many parts of the world are just a few examples.

But some Untouchables have followed their own paths.

My grandmother was able to triumph over seemingly impossible hardships and torments by discovering her talents as an entrepreneur. The root of her success, as you'll discover shortly, was her compassion for others. The business opportunities she created for herself came through the desire to care for others, not to profit for herself.

My father's success stemmed from his thirst for knowledge, and his commitment to pursue his own education. But knowledge alone wasn't enough; he didn't truly succeed until he acquired wisdom, through the values of his new-found faith. Knowledge may tell you what to do, but wisdom tells you when to do it, providing you with a judgment and discretion. Wisdom is the difference between doing the right thing, versus doing things right.

My father was repeatedly told that, as an Untouchable, his dream of earning a college degree were impossible. Yet he not only pursued a college degree, he earned a PhD in biology. In doing so, he became the first of our caste to do so. Although pursuing his dream of finding a teaching position in America was obviously impossible, that dream also came true. And with an unlikely assist from President Richard Nixon, he was later able to bring his family to join him in America.

My father must have inherited his inability to understand the concept "impossible" from his mother, Subbamma, and he must have passed it on to me. I was also born an Untouchable. And I also sought to achieve things outside the narrow constraints of what is permitted to those of my caste. I came to America, enrolled in college classes, though my schooling had ended after the fifth grade. Despite having grown up without a penny in my pocket, I soon found myself as a senior corporate officer managing finances for a $385 billion bank. Later, I became an academic researcher and program director at the University of California, Berkeley—one of the most prestigious universities in the world.

My own path has been forged by taking advantage of the opportunities in front of me. Many people simply don't see the opportunities they have, refusing to believe they are real, or imagining barriers that don't exist. They might ask "How can you teach at Berkeley alongside Nobel laureates?" or "How can you be responsible for corporate accounting at a major bank without first being a CPA or having a basic degree in the subject?"

God chooses people based not on their ability, but because of their availability. I struggled a great deal before I was able to make myself available to God's calling. But once I did, I found that opportunities I hadn't believed could come to me became my destiny.

If you had told me when I was an eight-year-old Untouchable boy in the village of Mori what lay in store for me, I would have told you that such things were impossible. But if you'd asked me as a 25-year-old man, I might have told you that such things were inevitable.

When I was a boy, there was one transistor radio in our village. It generally sat high atop a tall oven used to bake bricks. From that lofty perch, it could be heard by many people throughout the village. Often, music would play over the radio, and people in the village danced to these joyous sounds. I remember that once the sound emerging from that small miracle of technology was the voice of a man named Neil Armstrong speaking to the world from the moon in 1969.

That transistor radio and the amazing sounds it brought directly into our community should have been impossible. Men walking on the moon? Also, impossible. But the histories of innovation and exploration tell us that both the radio and the moonwalk were inevitable.

AT&T had, in fact, invented the transistor technology that made such radio possible decades earlier, but had not taken steps to that would make it possible for consumer products (such as radios) to leverage it. Smaller companies—such as the struggling Japanese company called Sony—had the entrepreneurial spirit that caused them to take that critical leap of faith. Without that leap, our village would not have been able to marvel to the sound of men walking on the moon. (AT&T's delay in licensing its transistor technology deprived the world of perhaps a decade of the joy that a single transistor radio could bring to a small village like the one I grew up in.)

Decades later—as an adult, and as an academic—I made a return visit to my home village of Mori with a very specific mission in mind. My goal was to understand how places like Mori could harness their full potential and raise the quality of life for everyone in the village. I knew the stories of how my grandmother, my father, and I had forged our own path to a more fulfilling life, But I also knew that such stories of Untouchables rising beyond the expectations for our caste were rare exceptions. Yet I was confident that it was possible to introduce small changes into village culture and industry that would open doors for all.

If a single transistor radio could bring so much joy to our village, what might result if we consciously and systematically designed small, scalable innovations that act as catalysts for positive change?

This idea became the spark for my research and the development of the idea of Smart Villages.

Some people feel that society is, by and large, static. Human nature is constant, they believe, and human nature dictates how we live our lives. But the only thing that remains truly constant in our society is change. Throughout human history, we've seen small sparks trigger radical transformations in an instant. The industrial revolution. Tin cans for storing food. The invention of elevators that made skyscrapers possible which, in turn, made dense cities economically viable. The internet.

Before I began exploring ways to trigger transformations in the millions of villages around the globe, I was part of some academic explorations to see if the development of Smart Cities could transform the world. The goal was to explore whether building such cities in the developing world could help them leapfrog over decades of social evolution. Was it possible that they could use the new infrastructure that would not merely vastly improve their status quo, but also move them in various ways ahead of cities in the developed world?

The infrastructure of those cities was built centuries ago and is now crumbling. Consider for example, the subways beneath the skyscrapers of Manhattan or London that are nearly impossible to repair or replace; old municipal water systems that regularly expose citizens to toxic contaminants; or even the catacombs of Paris that serve as a reminder of a way of life before the emergence of modern cities.

The Smart City vision, to a large extent, stalled out. The billions of people living in villages don't really need massive, expensive, shiny new infrastructure, and the government and business interests needed to fund them greeted these ideas with a tepid response.

From my own boyhood, I knew that something as simple as a single transistor radio could provide an entire village with joy. I knew that, if designed appropriately, even very modest changes could transform these villages not into ultra-modern cities, but into more sustainable and fulfilling villages—Smart Villages, as we call them. After several years of research, testing, and analysis, it's become clear that the Smart

Village concept and the changes it will bring are not impossible. The Smart Village Movement is not merely possible—it's inevitable.

My professional journey has led me to realize that the Smart Village Movement will help lead 3.4 billion people to a better life. (You can read more about that in my book "The Road to Mori.") My own journey—and those of my father and grandmother—have helped me better understand how even the most downtrodden souls can find lives of greater opportunity and fulfillment than they would ever have thought possible.

Sometimes these pathways to a better life may seem to be merely symbolic triumphs over the torment that life appears to hold in store for them. But very often, symbols matter.

Let me offer an example of how symbols have shaped my own life. The names we Untouchables are given, for example, are constant symbolic reminders of our place in society. My family name was "Nalli," which roughly translates to the name of an Indian bloodsucking bedbug. Therefore, Untouchables typically use their name only for legal purposes. The name I used in school was the name my biologist father bestowed on me: Charles Darwin. Later, I adopted a name my grandmother wanted for me: Solomon.

When I meet an Indian, they immediately understand much about me from both my names. I have the Untouchable name, from which I can never fully escape. I now go by a name from the world of science, reflecting a departure from the dominant Hindu culture, coupled with a name honoring the Biblical king whose reign was marked by wisdom, rather than violence. In the United States, much of this significance is lost, although some have noted the almost diabolical incongruence of having a Biblical and a scientific name so close together (For those familiar with the Scopes Trial, it's almost like carrying around my own Clarence Darrow and William Jennings Bryant.)

While many see names as unimportant symbols, adopting a new name can make a powerful difference in one's life. Some Untouchables find spiritual freedom by embracing religions such as Buddhism and Christianity in which the notion of a caste system is anathema. The Buddhist principles of seeking harmony with the universe leave no room for something as divisive as a caste. In Christianity, the notion of repentance overrides the notion that people will be condemned for the remainder of their life (let alone for the duration of many future lives) to a fate dictated by the circumstances of their birth.

Another way that some Untouchables have triumphed over their "birthwrong" has been to seek opportunity beyond the Indian borders, creating businesses in a global marketplace that is unaware of, or indifferent to, their caste.

I have been blessed to have family members who have found ways to live beyond our caste. Their stories are tales of triumph over the torment they experienced from their first breath. Their stories have informed my professional journey and encouraged me to give back to my homeland in ways that I believe will scale and drive sustainable changes, and that will free many people from the circumstances that limit their lives.

Many people have encouraged me to share my history, and I've also felt compelled to capture the stories of my grandmother, my father, and my own journey on paper. These are stories filled with hardship and torment. But ultimately, they are stories of triumph. The transformational journeys that my father and grandmother experienced are nothing short of impossible, as you can imagine. Many times, when I have talked about the transformation that I'm trying to achieve in the daily lives of hundreds of millions of people through the Smart Village movement, I am told it is also impossible.

But I do not believe this. My own grandmother and father have taught me how important it is to ignore that word.

My family's unthinkable story of triumph over torment begins with my grandmother, Subbamma.

THE TRIUMPH OF COMPASSION

**My grandmother Subbamma Nalli, at the height of her
prosperity in Burma in 1932.**

From her birth, it was dictated that Subbamma's
life would be full of torment, and devoid of
opportunities for happiness. That may have been a fair
assessment of her early years, but she was a
determined soul who found ways to transcend what
life had in store for her.

Subbamma was born into poverty in the small
village of Mori in India in 1890. Her low-caste status
meant that she would live not just this life but multiple

reincarnations as an Untouchable. Her prospects were dismal. She was persecuted by local villagers who considered even looking upon an Untouchable to be a sinful act. The community she was born into was confined geographically to an undesirable region of fallow land—soil left uncultivated to restore its fertility. Merely walking through certain streets or drinking from certain wells could result in severe punishment.

Even at birth, she was a disappointment to her father; as a female, she would be little more than a liability for a dowry her father would be unable to afford. He offered her up as a child bride when she was six years old to Anandham, who was almost 20 years older than she. Subbamma does not remember her marriage; she grew up with her in-laws and served as a family slave. After she reached child-bearing age, she was discovered to be infertile. Her husband was the only son in his family, and her infertility meant he would be unable to carry on the family name. Her husband's family branded her as a karmic curse and she was physically and mentally abused by her parents-in-law.

No Hindu deity could save her from her plight. She worshiped morning and night, looking with despair on the faces of her statues of her beloved deities. She pleaded for her curse to be lifted, she called upon different deities from among the 330 million that many Hindus believe in.

After decades of this persecution, when she was in her late thirties, she was thrown out of the house. Anandham selected another woman to carry on his family name as a replacement for Subbamma. Barren and rejected, she went to her father, only to face rejection again. In addition to being rejected by her society, community, and family, she had also suffered unbearable physical pain in her uterus that did not cease for more than thirty years.

Her spirit broken, she decided to put an end to her life by drowning herself in the river. On the verge of drowning, she was rescued by a young English missionary, Charles Whitehouse, who happened to be passing by. He prayed for her, and her uterine pain went away instantly, never to return. From that moment she became a follower of Jesus.

In the midst of the despair she felt as a result of being rejected by her society and family, Subbamma found hope. Her journey to death had ended and a journey of life had begun. Reborn, she also found purpose. She would become a channel through which blessings would flow to the village of Mori—and beyond.

Charles became Subbamma's protector. He spoke to Anandham to reconcile the couple and taught them both how to read and write. Subbamma's husband was a diligent student and learned basic math from Charles that would later open doors for him in Burma.

But as Subbamma began to share her newfound hope in Jesus, she was now subjected to a new form of persecution, this time from the community that wanted to silence her story. The retribution quickly escalated: her house was burned down several times, her well was poisoned, her family's cattle were killed, and her life was threatened. But none of these torments stopped her from following Jesus. Like Joseph of the Old Testament, she faced many adversities in life, but clung to her new beliefs that had drawn her from the pit of hopelessness.

The Birth of an Entrepreneur

Subbamma and her newly educated husband fled to Burma to escape this persecution and the caste system. Many Untouchable men—like Anandham—found that the tyranny of the caste system confined them to menial labor life as a scavenger. Their search for dignified employment often drove these men to leave the country. Typically, their wives were left behind in India for various reasons. For example, Burmese customs of the day treated foreign women as prostitutes. Subbamma fled to Burma knowing full well that this stigma would be more bearable than the isolation and persecution she faced at home.

Their new life in Burma opened the doors to many opportunities. Freed from persecution and armed with her new-found faith, Subbamma who had been thought barren, conceived and gave birth to my father, Raju, and three other children.

Anandham, who could now do basic math and read and write simple words, was recruited by one of the ports in Burma where he supervised a crew of 200 men and managed their payroll. Subbamma, now also equipped with a basic education, viewed her new community through an entrepreneur's lens. Opportunity, she soon realized, was all around her.

First, she started an Indian restaurant for all the men who had left their wives behind. For the travelling ship workers, she started a pickling business to satisfy their cravings. There was no refrigeration, so she pickled Indian favorites like shrimp, fish, and vegetables. This later expanded into a box lunch program to accommodate men who couldn't afford much. She extended a "buy now and pay later" credit offer to the men. As the payroll accountant, Anandham could deduct what they owed from their wages, so Subbamma had no problem with uncollectable debts.

With a growing reputation as a trustworthy merchant, she was able to become a local bank for the Indian men in Burma. She even started her own finance company, earning a profit by lending money to her customers.

Subbamma and Anandham were a hardworking couple, who left no stone unturned in their entrepreneurial pursuits. He would go out drinking with the boys every night after a hard day's work. To keep him safe and at home, Subbamma started a small brewery that produced beer of a higher quality that other local brews.

Subbamma's homemade beer wasn't the only product that became fashionable in her new Burmese community. She introduced the Burmese women—who dressed topless—to bras and Indian sarees. She turned the locals into models for the garments she started making and selling and was soon successfully creating fashionable new apparel styles made from Indian textiles, becoming something of a "Coco Chanel" of Burma. Prior to her success in women's fashion, she had started a men's textile import business that supplied clothing and blankets for Indian men in Burma.

Compassion was at the root of all of Subbamma's entrepreneurial activities. In Burma, she saw Indian men who'd had to leave the wives who had fed and clothes them back at home. Driven by her concern for their well-being, she began providing decent meals for them, which turned out to be a viable business. (Indeed, many of the men she cooked for told her they'd never eaten so well in their lives!)

Her small operation feeding hungry coolies who needed sustenance for their hard work loading and unloading heavy bags of rice expanded into a restaurant. Likewise, with Subbamma's knack for brewing, she could offer these men a safe place to relax and enjoy a beer or two at the end their workday—away from prostitutes and others who were eager to part them from their hard-earned wages.

Subbamma's compassion also extended to the people she had left behind in India. Her small business importing fabrics to make clothes and linens for the workers in Burma gave her the opportunity to hire many people to work for her in Burma, paying the travel costs to take them away from the devastating conditions in India. These people sustained her various businesses—textiles, pickling, brewery, banking, and even a downtown grocery store that became hugely successful.

Decades later, the many people she had helped showed their appreciation and respect at her funeral; her casket was surrounded all day by people she had cared for, served as a midwife, given names to, provided a home to, adopted, and found spouses for. Everyone wanted to say something about how she had helped them in their lives.

So many people trusted her, in fact, that she had no problem operating a bank. Her customers already trusted her with their lives, their well-being, and their children; trusting her with their money was far easier. As her businesses grew, she was able to return to Mori, where she had the chance to show off her son, Solomon Raju, parading him around the village. She was also able to buy land—even from the landlords, who never sold property to Untouchables—and create business opportunities for making textiles to be shipped to Burma.

Selling land to an Untouchable had always been unthinkable—but a national economic crisis was leading many to think unthinkable thoughts. Many lands were parceled out and used by needy people to build homes.

Subbamma was one of the first people able to replace her old mud hut and build a tile house with brick walls, rivaling the homes of her landlords. She did this against many protests and death threats from the local Hindu community. When her husband returned from Burma, he was brought before the village elders and warned. He gave in and ran back to Burma; Subbamma remained in Mori and challenged the local landlords.

She was firm and adamant and gained much political and social influence from the support of local women. She supervised and completed the construction of her home before returning to Burma to resume her work. The actions of this spirited mother of four led the way for other Untouchables to build better tile shelters.

> *"Right is right, even if everyone is against it,*
> *and wrong is wrong, even if everyone is for it."*
> *attributed to William Penn*

The Road from Burma

In December of 1941, all of Subbamma's accumulated wealth was lost in flames in an instant when World War II broke out and the Japanese started bombing Burma. Her youngest was three months old.

As the bombs began falling without any warning, people ran as they were, leaving everything behind and taking refuge in the thick, swampy jungle. They never returned to retrieve what they might have been left of their belongings.

With her husband beside her, Subbamma could only save the baby in her arms, her two little girls, and her 11-year-old son (my father, her firstborn). Lost in the jungle for three months during heavy bombing, many wandered and died due to lack of food or were eaten by wild animals. Others were bitten by snakes or killed and raped by gangs of thieves exploiting the situation. She described it as the Valley of the Shadow of Death.

"Yea, though I walk through the Valley of the Shadow of Death, I fear no evil for Thou art with me."

She was determined to keep moving by foot through the jungles and toward the shores of Burma, in hopes of catching a ship back to India. On the way, her family took refuge in Buddhist monasteries and temples in the forests to keep safe. Being grateful to Jesus for how miraculously He had provided them with their daily bread while hundreds in her camp were dying off, she found a pastor among the refugees, and asked him to name her baby. He gave the infant the name Elijah. She gathered a group of people to offer her simple testimony to them: *"The Lord is my shepherd; I shall not want."* She told them how Jesus had somehow preserved her family, just as He provided for the Prophet Elijah by having ravens deliver food and sustenance during a famine.

She felt that the same Shepherd would deliver her to the green pastures and still waters.

While taking refuge in a shrine, she and her children were praying with their backs turned to idols—to the militant Buddhists, this was an offense punishable by death. They surrounded her family and drew their swords. Subbamma looked up at the swords pointed at the throats of her and her children and said, "Lord show me thy glory." She said that Jesus gave her a special utterance at that time; she was enabled to speak in the language of these men. Whatever she had spoken convinced the men to put the swords down and quietly leave.

"Thy rod and thy staff shall comfort me."

As the throng of refugees moved toward the sea, moving from camp to camp, they would hear sirens warning them that aerial bombing was imminent. They took shelter in foxholes or whatever shelter they could find. Even when the sirens blared, everyone in the group could hear Subbamma. She would lift up her hands and pray "Not here Lord! Not here Lord!" People pleaded with her and asked her not to lift her hands because they looked like barrel guns protruding out of the foxholes aimed at the airplane bombers. My grandfather was too embarrassed to be around her, so he would hide himself away from the scene as people admonished her.

Weeks later, the family—Subbamma's family and her sister's family—arrived at the shores of Rangoon only to learn that no ships would be going to India; they were told to head back into the jungle. They had lost a great deal of weight and suffered from dysentery and other illnesses. Her breastfed baby was close to death due to lack of milk and malnourishment.

At the prospect of returning to the jungle, Subbamma lost her composure, breaking down completely. She threw her baby on the sand and began to scream, putting sand in her own hair. (As in the Old Testament, the women in Subbamma's time would put ashes in their hair as a sign of despair, when all hope was lost.) Many bystanders and army officers came to console her and remove her, but she wanted to die. Her faith in Jesus no longer made sense to her.

But as she was being removed from the shore, a man came walking by, and everyone stopped. He said, "I can help you." She looked up at this stranger and said, "Who are you? Are you Jesus or a Man?" He invited her and her family to go to a white bungalow up on the hill the next morning. She never saw him again.

The next morning, she arrived at the "bungalow"—actually, a mansion—on the hill with her family and her 8-month pregnant sister, who (along with her sister's two children) she had been caring for along the journey. Her husband and her sister's husband were also present. She found herself standing in front of a British Lord who had learned her language—Telugu—while serving in India

He knew of her situation and asked how many were in her group. She said she was speaking on behalf on her family and her sister's family. The English gentleman arranged passage for the group on a ship meant for families of those working for the British. The ship would take them to a border town between Burma and India.

Subbamma never knew why she had been given this miraculous accommodation. Perhaps the man who had seen her and her baby in the sand had been moved by her sorrow and relayed her situation to the British Lord. In any event, she gave the tickets to her six-foot-tall husband for safekeeping. The news spread that he had them and one man deceived him into exchanging the tickets for fake ones on another ship that he claimed would take a more direct route to India. Subbamma was furious. She searched every tent and hunted this man down; when she found him, she ripped open his pants and pulled out the tickets from his underwear!

As they were boarding the ship the next day, a siren blew. As war planes began to drop bombs, the ship began to pull away while the passengers were still loading. Many families were separated at that time. Both her husband and her sister's husband were not on the ship. As the ship began to move away, Subbamma went up to the captain and insisted that the ship be delayed by one minute as a special order from the British Lord. She had papers in hand to prove her relationship to him. It was just enough time for the two men to jump on before setting sail.

Still, many families—children, parents, and spouses—were separated. Subbamma told me that the tears, lamentations, and loud wailing continued for rest of the journey. Some jumped off the ship and drowned in the water as the only way to escape their distress.

After several days, they landed in Chittagong, a border town between India and Burma. Once on land at the border, they showered for the first time after three months and ate food provided for them by the refugee camps. They found their way to the next boat and, after some foot travel, boarded a train intended for war refugees. This train was packed like sardines. India was fighting for Independence from Britain, there was widespread rioting, and everyone was fighting for their lives. The trains were a microcosm of these ongoing tensions; there were battles fought for every square inch on the train, and many were trampled to death.

It was on this train that Subbamma's pregnant sister went into labor. Subbamma had children under her care and the two husbands proved useless in this situation. The crowds in the train could not take the screaming; an enraged policeman hit her sister in the stomach, causing her water to break. One man finally helped stop the train. It was midnight when they were ejected from the train in the middle of nowhere.

There were no lights as they weakly limped into utter, sprawling darkness. They walked to a small village facility and pleaded for medical help, someone who could pull the baby out and save the mother (as the water had been broken for some time). But nobody would be able to get there in time.

While holding her own infant in her hands and minding the other children, Subbamma managed to help her sister go into labor and give birth to a beautiful baby girl. The mother and child both lived and, as she had done with many newborns in India, Subbamma gave the baby its name: Elizabeth. Elizabeth would later become a registered nurse and would thank Subbamma for giving her life.

Creating a New Life at Home

With a newborn added to the group, the family returned to Mori—first by train, and then by foot for the last several hundred miles. The locals had written off Subbamma's family as war casualties. Indeed, many had hoped that Subbamma would never return as she caused much conflict with the higher caste. They were surprised to see the whole family walk back safely into the village.

Alas, Subbamma again faced the familiar caste problem as she sought employment to sustain her family. But she found a loophole through those injustices by way of her a talent for knitting beautiful lace products. No one in India would buy such products from an Untouchable, but she proposed a new business model: a business partnership with a missionary friend who would help export some of her lace samples to Great Britain.

It worked. Within months, she was getting orders for thousands of units and became the largest employer in the region. These dirt-poor Untouchables began to make some money from external sources. It was like manna from heaven.

Subbamma later established many other businesses using the cash flow generated by her lace exports to the UK. She began to prosper once again even though India as a nation was, for the moment, losing the fight for independence from Britain. She established a church, a school, started processing cashews, opened a birthing center and children's center, and sold food products in the Mori marketplace. In the market, she showed her generosity by adding extra for each customer, whether it was rice, mango, or milk. Her stall became a favorite.

She gave her products generously, but she gave her advice freely as well. She commissioned all the idle people in the village to do something productive, so much so that people would sometimes hide when they saw her walking down the path. Her collaborations benefited the local landlords and merchants who once had persecuted her family. She began to earn their respect because she employed over 50 people, and they profited greatly from the businesses she created for herself and the community.

"Thou preparest a table before me in the presence of mine enemies: thou anointest my head with oil; my cup runneth over."

During an earlier visit to Mori, Subbamma had started a church, which she expanded to include an orphanage and a refuge for unwanted women and children, a birthing center, and a school.

Her church fed souls and stomachs each week through her inspiring messages and home-cooked meals. She encouraged everyone to go to church, and eagerly lent her sarees to destitute women who had nothing but rags to wear. (She had many sarees for this reason.) She hosted Bible studies on the veranda of her house throughout my childhood. That same location is now called Subbamma House and is now part of the campus of Riverside School. Her house was burned down ten times but was rebuilt each time. The kitchen she used to feed the village is still there. She continued to serve the community with her husband until a ripe old age.

After Anandham passed away in 1972, she served the Mori community for another eight years, finally retiring from the daily chores at her orphanage in India to join her eldest son in San Francisco. But even after arriving in the United States, she did not stop knitting her lace. She sold her products in flea markets to support her people in India. She could not be in Mori anymore to personally bathe and feed the children in the orphanage as she once had but continued to support them through her lace. She could not sit idle knowing there were others she could serve.

Lessons from My Grandmother

When I reflect on Subbamma's life from the perspective of my current role as a professor at a leading business school, I see several remarkably current lessons about the role of entrepreneurship in society.

Many people today assume that entrepreneurs are driven solely by a profit motive. But Subbamma's businesses all grew out of her desire to help others—to feed them, provide them with clothes to wear, offer them a safe place to relax after a long day of work, to empower other businesses by trading with them, to provide employment to those who had few options in their lives.

Subbamma endured many hardships herself, which gave her a deep understanding of the people in her community who eventually become her customers.

She did everything she could to help others in her community, long before that compassion evolved into business opportunities. Her compassion fueled the growth of those businesses. Her decisions were rooted in her care for others—the customers, the suppliers, the distributors and employees—her motive was never to maximize a return on investment. In times when she was able to generate a profit, her earnings went back to the community she loved, not into a luxurious lifestyle or an early retirement.

As Subbamma's experiences demonstrate, entrepreneurship can be a powerful equalizer. The notion of equality is at the heart of the notion of commerce: Any transaction involves a buyer and a seller who exchange goods or services because they agree that those goods and services are of equal value. That process can overcome deeply rooted social forces. When times get tough in India, landowners who would never think of selling property to an Untouchable found themselves willing to sell if the price was right. For her part, Subbamma didn't hold grudges against them; she focused on the good she was able to do for her community.

Compassion sparked her business, drove their growth, allowed competitors to become partners, and enemies to become friends. It created a brand identity for her businesses that never tarnished—and that her customers and beneficiaries never forgot.

Subbamma hoped her oldest child—my father—would someday continue her business endeavors and continue to use those businesses as a way to help others and provide for the community. But she didn't fully appreciate a different aspect of her legacy. Although my father wasn't inclined to follow in her entrepreneurial footsteps, he found his own path to overcoming the circumstances he was born into. My father's education would become a powerful force in his life, for better and sometimes for worse. Subbamma didn't realize that the son who had worked for her as an errand boy would impress a local mill owner, who would later encourage him to pursue lofty academic goals.

That path led him to become separated from his own family, pursue a distinguished academic career and, with the surprising intervention of President Richard Nixon, be reunited with his family in America.

THE TRIUMPH OF WISDOM

My father Dr. Solomon Raju, at commencement at the Scripps Institution of Oceanography in 1966.

My father, Solomon Raju, was born in Burma in 1930, after Subbamma and Anandham had gone there to escape the tyranny of the caste system and make a living. They named him after King Solomon out of their hope that he, too, would grow up to be a wise leader.

Shortly after he was born, Subbamma took him to church and "auctioned" him. This was a tradition intended to demonstrate how thankful you are for your child, while making a donation to the church. At the auction, Subbamma bid 30 pieces of silver—the same price Jesus was "sold" for— to claim her son back. (She was never at risk of losing her son, as no one in the village had the means to outbid her.)

While my dad was still a child, Subbamma put him to work in several of her businesses. He ran all kinds of errands, such as delivering jars of pickles or textiles by rickshaw and returning with the money they sold for. He might also help out in her bank, grocery store, brewery, or restaurant. His childhood days and years were filled with work. When his two younger sisters were born, Solomon Raju's work doubled: His mother's businesses were expanding and that meant he had to care for his sibling while also completing a growing number of household chores.

Subbamma's customers were primarily the Untouchable men who had escaped the caste system by making their way to Burma for a life of physical labor, loading and unloading ships at the harbor. But my father was told by his parents that their situations—and his—were much better than in India. Back home, they

44

were lorded over by the landlords and lived in segregated communities, where they were assigned dirty and degrading tasks that only members of the Untouchable caste were expected to do.

When my dad had just turned 12, his mother gave birth to another son. He loved his baby brother and was protective of him, caring for him and watching over him all day long while his mother was busy overseeing business operations. His brother made his life blissful, and he played with him while doing the household chores his mother assigned him. Even while he did housework, he would assist with Subbamma's various businesses—accepting and parceling out deliveries or mixing dough for the roti.

When the baby turned three-months-old in late 1941, Japanese bombs began to fall on Burma as World War II broke out. The family fled into thick swampy jungles of Burma, without looking back or running back to pack their clothes. For months, my father lived in fear, unsure if he'd live to see the next minute. He saw death all around him as his family and other refugees kept moving deeper into the jungle. They sought shelter in trenches to escape the bombs as sirens blew, but there were many casualties. They stepped over the bodies of people who had died of starvation, snake bites, and attacks by wild animals.

He hung on to his mother, brother, and his two little sisters while his mother carried her baby and went days without food or shelter. The sound of people wailing surrounded them, and Subbamma would often fasten their Indian village address to his clothes so he could find his way home if the rest of them died. She also made him hide in a separate trench from his brother and sister for similar reasons.

He would hear the bombs go off and feel the fear and anguish that he and other members of his family would continue to relive for many years, even into adulthood. But his heart was also filled with gratitude for his family's survival; many others who travelled with them had not been so fortunate. He saw many children become separated from their parents, saw families lose loved ones, and witnessed many horrific atrocities.

After three months, the family reached the sea and were extremely fortunate to get on the last ship to the border town of Chittagong, located between India and Burma in what is now Bangladesh. When they disembarked, they began the harrowing train journey that would take them closer to Mori. On that journey, many were thrown out of the moving trains and left to die in the darkness of night. It was under such circumstances that my father witnessed his maternal aunt, who limped along with them throughout this journey, go into labor in the train. Subbamma ended up pulling the infant from her sister's womb as she held on to her own starving baby.

After several more train rides, they were kicked off the train for travelling without tickets. Their refugee voices went unheard. They went by foot to a bus, and later traveled again by foot, finally returning to Mori in February, 1942. My father was the first one to joyously announce to everyone that they were not dead, as had been feared—but very much alive. Not everyone was eager to welcome them home. Many relatives had moved into our family's home during our absence and were not happy to see our family return. This began a feud that would continue for some time.

My father and his family returned to their own home—the segregated and isolated village designated for Untouchables—as refugees. Their village was surrounded by higher caste communities that treated them as lower than human beings. Solomon Raju felt that his caste was his destiny, that his life was already defined by karma, and he should not hope for anything better. But my father had grown up in Burma— where there was no caste system. Having known a different way, he was keenly aware of and frustrated by this injustice.

Arriving in Mori at the age of 12, my father made friends with other boys and sometimes wandered into the homes of his higher-caste playmates. This caused an uproar in the community. One day he sat in a chair in someone's home, not realizing that Untouchables were not considered worthy of entering the homes of the higher castes, let alone of sitting on their chairs. This left a mark on him that would haunt him later in life.

He continued to help his mother continue her entrepreneurial activities despite the constraints of her place in the caste system and the lordship of higher castes. His hardworking mother took on cashew processing contracts by employing large numbers of women. This job was left for the Untouchables, as the processing units generated many toxic emissions, that caused skin and respiratory problems. He helped her in many of her side businesses, such as selling rice and groceries in the local market. She ran a very tight ship as the largest employer in her village.

A Passion for Learning

A prominent rice mill owner with whom Subbamma traded was a Brahmin who also happened to be a senior teacher in a local private school. He noticed that my dad was a bright and handsome young man whose talents were being squandered as he toiled away in manual labor, day and night, to help his mother. This good-hearted Brahmin man took interest in the young boy, persuaded Subbamma to apply for him to attend the school and offered to admit him there.

When my father showed up to class as the first Untouchable boy to attend school, he was interrogated by a teacher responsible for admission. The teacher did not want to admit him, so she told the senior Brahmin teacher that the boy was useless—a hopeless Untouchable. The senior teacher insisted that my father had the intelligence to learn very quickly and be allowed to stay. Thanks to his persuasion, this eager student started going to school at age 13.

However, my dad was well aware of the unfair treatment he received. Teachers would not touch him or come close to him. When they handed him an object, such as chalk for writing on the board, they would put it on the table—but he was not allowed to pick it up if their hand was still on it. He was ridiculed by other students and even his teachers if, for example, he asked questions to help him understand things he had never learned about.

Despite this hostile environment, my father was passionate about learning and would come home and teach others what he had learned. He held class for the local children in the evenings on his home veranda. This was the beginning of a school in Mori village. As a student, he did well and completed high school. He was frustrated that his people were not provided educational privileges. Many years later, Subbamma donated a piece of land on which my dad helped build a small mud-hut school where many children studied, including me. There was no infrastructure, just a roof to protect us from the hot sun. Kids sat on the dirt floor, and the sand in front of us served as slates for practicing writing and reading.

In 1950 the new Indian constitution written by Dr. B. R. Ambedkar (himself an Untouchable) at the request of Mahatma Gandhi, gave Untouchables a few privileges, such as the right to education. But the cost of college remained prohibitive. However, my grandmother had conceived of a business that would free her from the shackles of the local landowners so that she could finally be her own boss; she found a way to access more lucrative markets by exporting handmade lace products to England through her local missionary friends.

She was soon training many women to make lace and became the largest employer in the village. This also created more demand for labor in the cashew business since many women switched to lace production. Her financial success meant that she was able to send her daughters, my father, and, later, his younger son, to college.

After entering college, my father was exposed to new ideas about different kinds of social structures. He was disillusioned by the inequities he had faced; he found like-minded thinking when he became a Communist, which he believed reflected his pursuit for a more just way of life for himself and for the overall community. He attended Communist rallies in secret;

much of the activities of the Communists took place "underground." Because embracing Communism meant renouncing the Hindu religion, he denounced his belief in God, rejected his Christian name of Solomon, and began to use the secular name, Soma.

My father completed his bachelor's degree in Biology at Andhra Christian College, which was run by Lutheran missionaries and accepted Untouchables. As he was returning home to Mori, not knowing what he would do with his degree, he happened to sit next to a Brahmin professor who taught the sciences at Narsapur College, across the river from Mori. Prof. Rama Sharma also happened to be a Communist sympathizer and a progressive thinker, so they bonded right away. (Although there was much hostility toward Communists among members of the higher castes and more dominant religions, intellectuals were more tolerant of their ideas.)

Knowing that my father was looking for a job, the professor asked him many questions and quizzed him on various topics. He was impressed with my father's knowledge of the sciences and offered him post under him as a lecturer at the college.

He later told my father that many Brahmins applied for the job, but he chose my father due to his sweeping knowledge of the subject matter. My father would later recount the many good people who appeared in his life and the help they provided, for which he was very grateful.

My father was married in 1953 to his first cousin, a 14-year-old woman selected for him by Subbamma. He insisted on a small Communist-style marriage. He was a 22-years-old lecturer at the Narsapur College, and just beginning his PhD studies. I was born in August of 1954, the year my mother turned 15. My father named me Charles Darwin in hopes that I would prove the theory of evolution as a definitive fact.

He sent his wife (my mother) to a Communist camp to learn the sewing trade to earn her living while he was away teaching and studying. This arrangement separated me from her as a child, so my grandmother took the lead in raising me. I became closer to my grandmother, but still longed for my mother, who only visited me once a month for a few hours. Growing up, my father was never there for me as he was away dealing with his own struggles—not just his pursuit of an academic career, but also the health issues that later plagued him.

My father did well in college, graduating with honors, and hoped to attend medical school. Unfortunately, he did not have enough money to apply. Professor Rama Sharma's father-in-law, Sri Pada Laxmi Narasimham, a prominent attorney who fought on behalf of the Communists, helped my father to get into a master's program at Andhra University, where both his son and son-in-law were working at that time.

My dad completed his master's degree with honors and was later admitted into a PhD program.

This was an astonishing accomplishment for an Untouchable—but he still regrets not having the chance to pursue a medical career. He would have been a compassionate doctor who would have taken great care of his patients.

Crises, Disappointments, and Miracles

During the final year of his PhD program, my father started coughing up blood and was diagnosed with an advanced case of tuberculosis by the university physician. He was referred to the King George Hospital in Vizag where a series of X-rays determined that one of my father's lungs would need to be removed to prevent further deterioration of the other lung, which was also infected. Even more dire was that his doctors did not offer much hope that he would make it through the six-hour surgery.

My father wrote his last testament to my mother, who had been told to stay away from him to avoid risk of catching the disease. In his last testament, he instructed her to stay dedicated to her training to be a tailor, as she would need it to her to earn enough money to take care of me. Subbamma knew that nothing is impossible for God, so she travelled to Vizag and pleaded with him to cancel the surgery, as she knew that

God could renew his lung. The same God that opened her womb could perform a miracle in her son's life.

He considered Subbamma to be an uneducated and uninformed woman, swept up by her emotions. But just before the surgery, as they walked together to the operating room, my dad turned around to say goodbye to his mother. Subbamma told him, "All you have to say is 'Jesus'." My father broke down and said "Jesus."

He immediately felt a bolt of energy come into him. He thought he was healed and told the doctors that he would not go through with the surgery. The doctors told him he was making a foolish mistake and reminded him what the X-rays had revealed about his deteriorating lung. After returning to his living quarters at the university, my father began to have doubts and couldn't sleep. At midnight, he heard a loud voice in the room declare, "You are healed." He woke up and found his mother sleeping on the floor next to him. He asked her if she heard the loud voice. She had not.

He left his room and went out into the hallway, checking each room next to him. The hospital was a teaching hospital and it was summer; the students had gone home, and the building was nearly empty. It was on that day that my father accepted God and became a follower of Jesus. He found a new Master.

Growing up in Vizag—my family moved from the Mori village to Vizag in 1963—I saw my father striving to emulate the actions of Jesus, his new Master. He established the first Christian fellowship at Andhra University, which took on social projects to help people in need. I remember him going every week to care for the families in the local fishing village. He was mentor, advisor, facilitator, tutor, and teacher to many people too numerous to mention individually. He made time for people and was a great role model for me.

I remember building our thatched hut in Vizag—a basic shelter with mud walls and a dirt floor —with our own hands. Our modest two-room home was always full of people. My parents housed many others in the little space we had. Our house was like an overcrowded inn— sometimes it even felt more like a stable with people in it instead of cattle. Many people flocked to our home to receive advice from my father and seek direction for their lives, and my mother was a great hostess. We shared with our guests and relatives what little we had; I remember that we often only had one meal a day, as that was all the food we could afford for ourselves.

In 1966, my family faced a difficult transition. We went to my father's commencement, held in an open-air auditorium. We were proud that he was the first Christian Untouchable man to graduate with a PhD. from an Indian University. I ran to the auditorium and took a seat, only to be asked to leave by the men in charge. I explained that my father was graduating with a PhD. Once they found out his name and who he was, they told me that I was a Mala, an Untouchable, and would not be able to sit there.

I was asked to stand and watch from across the street. I stood across the road with my aunt, mother, and brother as my father's name was called by the governor of the state. As the names were called one by one, there was a great applause from the crowd as they received the diplomas. When my father's name was called and as he walked up to the stage—the proud moment that I was waiting for—no one clapped. There was no applause.

Rather than feeling proud of my dad, I felt sad for him. He had achieved so much in the face of countless adversities and great obstacles—but his accomplishments were appreciated by so few.

We returned home on foot to our thatched hut with the diploma in my dad's hand. I remember telling others visiting our home that he had no future, that he could never get an appointment at the university because of his caste. One of his foreign PhD advisors suggested that he apply abroad, where such things are merit-based. And one day my father brought home a big catalogue from the university library that had names of American universities.

As my father wrote out the addresses on envelopes, I remember licking stamps and pasting them onto envelopes late into the night under the kerosene lamp inside our little hut. We mailed out over a hundred resumes and letters inquiring about possible research positions. Many did not respond, and those that did reply sent regrets. Still, when the letters arrived, we would anxiously wait for my father to come home. We had grown accustomed to the disappointment and rejection that was delivered inside every letter.

Months later, an envelope arrived from the world-renowned Scripps Institution of Oceanography at the University of California in San Diego. I could read my father's feelings as he held this letter: Why would the top-ranked university in marine biology accept him when so many lesser-known universities rejected him? I thought that he would simply throw the letter away; but Subbamma, visiting us at the time, said to him: "God will always give you the best and not the second best."

My father was overcome by emotion as he opened and read the letter. It was from Dr. John D. Isaacs, head of the Oceanography Department, offering him a position at the University of California. When my father informed Dr. Isaacs that he would be unable to accept this astounding offer, as he had no money for travel, Dr. Isaacs responded by sending him an air ticket.

My father was finally being recognized for his worth, and by one of the top academic institutions in the world. He still treasures the letter he received from Dr. Isaacs and has saved it to this day. Later, my dad found out that his application letter was about to be tossed in the trash by the professor who received it at UCSD, but Dr. Isaacs appeared in the nick of time and asked what was being discarded.

He was told that it was from someone who was doing research on eels in the Indian Ocean—discovering, cataloging and discovering new species. Dr. Isaacs was intrigued. He had a goal of identifying all the species on the planet, and they had barely scratched the surface.

I always felt that God's hand was upon my dad in all the details of his life. When my father left for America, it was an amazing experience for us. When went to see him off, it was our first time we had ever seen an airplane up close. No one from our village had ever flown to America in an airplane. My father shed many tears as he was leaving and saying goodbye to us, his tears mixing his joy for the opportunity, his sorrow for the separation, his anxiety about what would come next, and his gratitude for the blessings bestowed upon him.

A Family Reunited

We didn't see my father for four years, but he stayed in touch with me by sending postcards and describing life in the United States. He was concerned about my education, as I had been dismissed from several schools. I was failing grades again and again, repeating the same classes because I had never learned the basic foundations at my mud-hut Mori school. I started staying home because no formal school would accept me.

My father arranged for tutors to teach me, but that did not work either; the tutors just took the money and had no interest in my education. These tutors were from a higher caste and treated me as someone who lacked the intelligence to learn. My father's letters expressed his anxiety about my future; he wrote pages and pages about what and how I should study.

In 1969, my father's visa was due to expire; he was supposed to return to India when his term of employment ended. As it happened, President Richard Nixon came to visit the La Jolla Presbyterian church in San Diego, which was the church my father attended. President Nixon was a personal friend of Pastor Evans, who was also an advocate for foreign students. Pastor Evans introduced Nixon to my father, and they had a brief chat about his situation. Shortly thereafter, President Nixon initiated a special provision for two months that allowed prominent scientists to apply for a green card.

My father applied during this narrow window of opportunity—he doesn't even recall how he found out about it, and he knew many other scientists who missed this opportunity. But as a result of this intervention by the president, he was able to establish permanent residency, for himself as well as his entire family.

(There is certainly an element of irony in the fact that my grandmother was rescued by a man named Whitehouse, and my father's destiny was changed by the president of the White House. I myself am still awaiting an assist from the Oval Office, although I have had the privilege of sitting with, and providing advice to, the president of my native country.)

Before his term ended at UC San Diego, my father saw an ad in a periodical for the position of biology professor and head of the Department of Science at Simpson University in San Francisco (it is now located in Redding). He applied and secured the job immediately. He returned to India to bring us all back to the United States, which was now possible thanks to the intervention of President Nixon.

My father published many research papers in prestigious journals and discovered dozens of new marine species (one was even named after my mom, Monognathus jesse, and one was named for Dr. Isaacs, Monognathus isaacs). He also won several awards during his tenure at Simpson, including the Outstanding Educator of America Award in 1976.

Lessons from My Father

Abraham Lincoln said, "Nearly all men can stand adversity, but if you want to test a man's character, give him power." This quotation could be referring to my father. He has achieved much and gained prominence, and his character was sorely tested over time. Yet his heart is always filled with gratitude for those that helped him throughout his life.

He often speaks of those who made a crucial difference in it, including: his parents; Dr. John D. Isaacs, the senior Brahmin teacher who admitted him to school; Professor Rama Sharma the Brahmin professor, and Sri Pada Laxmi Narasimham the attorney, who recommended him to the PhD. program; the two Brahmin doctors (Dr. Marthana Sastry, MD, FRCS, the university physician, and Dr. Krishna Murthy, MD, MS, the prominent surgeon at the King George Hospital);

Mr. Venkatapathy, the Mori landlord who loaned him money to cover the expenses for his trip to the U.S.; and Charles Whitehouse, who prayed for his mother to conceive so he could be born as a gift from God to his barren mother.

Above all, he thanks God for saving his life by giving him new lungs and, most importantly, a new heart that enabled him to respond to people with the compassion of Jesus. In 1986, my father founded the Project India Compassion trust in India which is dedicated to providing education and medical care, primarily to Untouchables, which opens doors for many children in the village. This project continued the work begun by his mother, Subbamma, and I would later follow in their footsteps.

From my father, I learned the value of education—as well as its hazards. King Solomon said that too much knowledge can bring grief. And, indeed, my father's education led him to Communism, which caused him to live a period of his life "underground," separated from his family and community. A formal education gave him awareness of the world, but not wisdom. It was only when he began to follow Jesus that he found a purpose in his life. He learned to never give up, and to always move forward. It took me a while but eventually, I learned similar lessons from him. My father also learned—and taught me, through his example—the importance of gratitude, and never forgetting the people who helped him over the years.

Compared to my father's day, education—which is a foundation for creating more equitable opportunity for all—is now greatly facilitated through digital technology. It is easy to access, mobile, less expensive, easy to keep current, available 24/7, and offers a broader range of virtual courses. Students today aren't limited to practicing their reading and writing in the sand; knowledge flows like water moving from high to low and everywhere in between, with no need for physical libraries.

This generation is blessed with many tools that are readily available, and often free. How we use this power and what we do with it will test the character of this generation.

My dad has accomplished so much, far beyond any reasonable or even unreasonable expectations. But he felt there was one aspect of his life in which he'd been unsuccessful: his oldest son, me. He often said I was the biggest disappointment in his life. He'd hope I'd pursue the medical degree he'd been unable to achieve for himself. But through his mentorship—and the guidance of Subbamma and Jesus, whom I now follow—I finally found my own path to overcoming the torments of my Untouchable heritage.

I never became a doctor as my father hoped, but today I hire doctors. I never became the entrepreneur that Subbamma would have liked me to be, but today I teach Silicon Valley engineers and leading corporate executives around the globe. And while I have never been a preacher, my curious name has given me the opportunity to change the thinking of religious scholars and practitioners.

THE TRIUMPH OF DESTINY

The author, Solomon Darwin, at age 16, before leaving India for the United States in 1970.

I first set foot on American soil on September 13, 1971, when we arrived in Francisco. My father had the opportunity to bring his family to the U.S., but I didn't want to leave India. I knew that I would not be able to cope with the challenges that America would bring into my life.

America was the "Land of Opportunity," but what opportunities could there be for someone who was utterly unprepared and unqualified? Having grown up in a segregated village, I suffered from low self-esteem—or perhaps it was merely a case of accurate self-esteem. I had just turned seventeen but at best, my level of education was at a fifth-grade level. I could barely read and write English, and I did not know other subjects beyond that. I only had my poor education from a village school for Untouchables where I couldn't make the minimum marks to advance to the next grade.

It was constantly demoralizing to be the foreign boy from the remote village of Mori, India, now sitting in a city school in America surrounded by much younger students who all seemed to have no problems with their classes. This consistent stress and failure—coupled with a complete lack of self-worth—led to dark thoughts, including a failed suicide attempt.

For most of my childhood, I was separated from my parents and was raised by my grandmother in the village of Mori. I was sent to a segregated school for the lowest caste: a simple thatched hut with no walls, located in the center of the village. All grades were taught under one roof with no textbooks, notebooks, or slates. We were told to write the Indian alphabet in the sand with our fingers. I learned nothing beyond the alphabet until I was eight years old. Most of the time, the teacher did not show up; when he did come, he came to pass the time rather than actually teach. I didn't enjoy school, and I didn't learn much.

My mother was gone most of the time. My father had sent her off to live far away in a Communist camp to learn the sewing trade, so that she could support me while he was off to college. The training took some time, as the students had to take turns at the school's few sewing machines. Whenever she came to visit me, she also had to work an extra day to pay for her travel costs and for the treats she would bring me. I don't remember knowing what my father was like when I was young. I remember when my mother told me that he was suffering from tuberculosis in Vizag and might not have long to live. My grandmother, Subbamma, loved me and cared for me, but I grew up being depressed most of the time.

Because my parents were absent for much of my childhood, I assumed that most children were motherless. I was told that I would often ask people around me if the birds and other animals we saw near our home had a mommy. This question often puzzled the adults. When my grandmother took me to the Mori market, it made me sad to see many little children my age begging for food and money—many were handicapped and had sores and other injuries. I would ask my grandmother to explain what had happened to them and where their mother was.

As a boy, I also felt the discrimination and scorn that Untouchables are subjected to. One incident stands out in my mind as a vivid contrast between the innocence of childhood and the bigotry of the culture I was born into. We had a baby calf that was born right in front of me. I eagerly watched it emerge from the womb. It became my friend; the calf knew who I was, and we had fun chasing each other around. Sometimes we veered into the rice fields that belonged to the landlords who lived adjacent to our home. When this happened, I would hear screams of outrage that I was contaminating their land just by walking on it, especially the temple property on the corner of the intersection. They chased me away, saying that they would kill my calf if I did it again. I began to live in fear of my immediate neighbors.

Separation and Longing

Once in a blue moon, I was told that my mom would be coming the next day to visit me. I would stay awake all night anxiously waiting for the sun to rise. Once there was light, I would stand on the veranda that overlooked the rice fields and wait for her to appear at the end of the narrow path that connected to the main road. As soon as I saw her, I ran as fast as my little bare feet could carry me, ignoring the many thorns that pricked them along the way. I was always out of breath when I finally fell into her arms. My mom cried even louder than I as we embraced one another in the middle of the road.

She would always bring me paisley shaped biscuits, but those treats brought me no comfort. My first words to her upon our embrace were always "Don't go away again," and she would console me by saying that she would stay this time. I held her hand tightly and led her back to our home to show off my mom to everyone. These were the happiest moments in my young life. However, by late afternoon, she would disappear suddenly. I would go house to house searching for my mom.

After many hours, as night came, someone would tell me that she had left in secret, as she could not bring herself to say goodbye to me. I would always ask when she would return, and always heard the devastating answer "not for a while." This news would throw me into a deep depression for many days despite the love and comfort from my grandmother. This pattern of my mother coming and leaving played out the same way many times.

Eventually, I knew that it wasn't true when she told me that she would stay this time, but I still asked the question anyway, just to hear her answer. I would also try to be more watchful, hoping I could stop her from leaving if I kept my eye on her. But she always managed to steal away. It was devastating for me as a child to have my hopes dashed time and again. I grew weary of the cycle of crushed dreams and lost any desire to live.

My grandmother, Subbamma, was the only source of comfort to me during that time. She often held me and cried with me for hours. She would ask me to pray that my father would not die and that my mother would return. I was the apple of her eye, always with her; we cuddled at night in the same cot. However, I wanted my mother and nothing else would fill that deep longing. I loved my mom. She was a beautiful young lady, and I later found that she was only fourteen when she conceived me.

There was so much grace about her, and I felt very secure when she was around me. From the moment she arrived, she would start attending to everyone in the home and doing chores for her mother-in-law—washing clothes, doing dishes, cooking, and serving food. She was the most selfless and nurturing woman I have ever known to this day. She was like a servant who cared for everyone around her, putting aside her own grief about the separation from her baby and the husband who, at the time, she thought was dying.

Only much later did I realize that she had to obey my dying father's request to learn a trade, and that her training was being offered freely by the Communist network that sought to liberate people by equipping them with valuable skills. Our separation was not a choice but a necessity, so she could learn the skills she needed to support us so that we could survive after my father was gone.

I don't know how or when my deep longing for my mother developed. But I felt a powerful bond, and her absence left a vacuum in my heart and a longing that could not be quenched. Later in life, I realized that I was built this way by my Maker; it was my genetic disposition. I was made a certain way.

Today, I see the same bond in my youngest daughter who can't live without her mom. She latches onto her and cuddles her as she lays down to sleep at night. My son, Judah, was the same. Growing up, he would always seek me out and want to be held. Until he was eight years old, and too heavy to carry, he would cuddle me tightly throughout the church service

One summer day, when Judah was only two, I was teaching in France and my wife, Amy, brought him to the university. He saw me at the end of the long hallway and came running up to me as fast as his feet could carry him with his hands raised, poised to be picked up. When we embraced, I shed a few tears for the baby I once was and grieved for that baby back in Mori, cherishing the precious relationship he had with his mom.

This is how I was made. My deepest longings were for a special relationship with a mother who had been kept far away from me for reasons beyond her control. As I matured and grew, that longing for a relationship with my mom evolved into a longing for Jesus, whom I now follow. I developed a personal relationship with Jesus whose presence I felt through my mom and grandmother. My grandmother read many stories about Jesus to me, and I wanted to emulate him as best I could.

He has been my role model for the style of servant leadership that Jesus practiced, an approach I was first exposed to by my mother and grandmother. I chose Jesus as my "Guru" and have become his follower. I now feel His presence through the deepest valleys of my journey.

Being Tested in America

When I was eight years old, we moved from the Mori village to Visakhapatnam, where my father was completing his PhD program. The informal education I had received back in Mori had left me completely unprepared for schools where the students were actually expected to learn. I failed the entrance exams at each school I was sent to and was also dismissed from a private school that my father thought might be what I needed.

This was about the time my father left to begin a university position in America. I had no guidance, and no school would accept me. I was finally sent to another private school, but they couldn't help me make up for all of the years I'd missed. What I really needed was one-on-one instruction.

My confidence was at its lowest level, and I got into a lot of mischief to draw attention to myself. My mother was frustrated with me, but my grandmother felt that I could do no wrong. She often used to say that God was preparing me to be a tool in His hand to serve people, although I didn't believe her. However, even at this young age, I had a strong sense there was a purpose for which I was made, even if I hadn't yet figured out what it could be.

When I was feeling down or when troubles came my way, my sadness—and my lack of purpose—often left me feeling there was no value to my life. Once, as a small boy, I found some DDT pesticide powder and decided I would eat it and end my suffering. That day, I said goodbye to the other students at my school. But one little kid told me that God would never forgive me, and that he was sad that he wouldn't see me in Heaven.

That interaction stopped me. I was only a boy in the third grade, but I had a longing to be right with God. Being separated from my father and cast out from school left me with no one else to rely on, and I developed a closer relationship with Jesus who brought comfort and hope to my life.

Sadly, that little first-grader who saved my life was later murdered.

After four years, my father returned to bring us to America. My level of education hadn't improved, and I didn't want to go to the United States. He said that I had no choice in the matter. I remember going into our outhouse toilet (as there was no privacy with a house full of people) and praying on my knees: "Dear Jesus, give me pain throughout my life, a thorn in my flesh, that I will keep on my knees so that I will not cease to follow you after going to America." I was afraid that the abundance of America might lead me astray. I didn't know what I was asking for at that time. But I knew that

His grace would be abundantly sufficient to help me along the path through the many difficulties I would face as I ventured into the future.

Upon settling down in our rented home in San Bruno, California (just outside San Francisco), I was too ashamed and too old at age seventeen to join a sixth-grade class, which is where, academically, I would have fit in. I finally braced myself and found the strength to enter the campus of Skyline College, the community college that was just blocks away from our home. Back then, the campus was full of hippies, and drugs were rampant. This environment scared me. The hippie mantra of "peace, love, and understanding" was all well and good, but the reality was that I was the only dark person walking around among so many white people who were also much bigger than I.

I approached the front desk and asked the lady there for an admission application. But because they didn't accept students without high school diplomas, she wouldn't give me one. I couldn't fight back the tears that welled up when I heard this disappointing news and began to walk away. As I went through a pair of double doors, she came running after me. "Let me see what I can do," she said. "I can see that you are a passionate young man."

She spoke to the dean of students, Dr. White, who allowed me to sign up for an admission test. The first question I asked her was "How much time do I have to prepare?" She said that I would only have two weeks. She instructed me to use this time wisely, as I would only be given that one opportunity.

I didn't even know how to begin. I didn't know basic math or any of the basic sciences. I went to the library every day and studied as hard as I could. I even had a few sympathetic hippie friends helping and encouraging me.

The day of the test arrived. When I returned through the double doors, the same lady handed me the test, saying "Take as much time as you like." To my surprise, the test was only about English and comprehension; a one-page article followed by some questions about it. I knew that I could handle it because

I knew how to speak and write English. I had not learned grammar yet but felt that I could at least pass.

After two hours, the lady returned, took my paper and left to grade it while I waited in the lobby. I felt pretty good and I prayed to Jesus to help me. The lady came back after thirty minutes, with some bad news for me. I scored only 35 out of 100; this was off the charts, as the passing grade was 70. I put my head down and shed many tears. She sat next to me and suggested that I find a tutor and enroll in high school to rectify my problems with English, along with my shortcomings in the other subjects.

Finally, I turned around and walked back out through the double doors. I was about to turn onto the main road when I once again heard the woman's voice behind me as she tried to catch her breath after running to catch up to me. She said that she had spoken again to Dean White, who had agreed to admit me conditionally; after a two-semester probationary period, he would assess my improvement and decide if I could continue. I thanked Jesus for this news and swore to myself that I would study day and night to succeed in the opportunity I had been given.

A generation later, in 2013, my son Judah was enrolled in the same college. He became the founder and president of the Public Speaking Club and invited me to be his first speaker. I was not too happy about this prospect, as it would surely bring back many bad memories. Judah jokingly said that it was too late— posters were already up in the hallways around the campus and, besides that, everyone loved my beard.

I wanted my father and my mother to be there as an inspiration to me, so I took them along to the presentation. The dean introduced me by reading the long resumé from my faculty page at UC Berkeley. I heard him say how honored the college was have one of its alumni back to share his story with them today, and then he introduced me as Professor Darwin, who has achieved so much in his life.

I began my presentation, addressing my remarks to the dean of the business school who was in attendance: "Sir, I started my academic life in the United States on this campus under the most adverse circumstances. I was admitted on probation. If you check your records, you will find that I was your poorest student. I believe that no student received as many D's and F's as I did. I also withdrew from many classes at the end of the semester, only to retake them again and again.

Despite my faith in Jesus, I could not cope, and thoughts of suicide were frequent. It took me more than three years to improve and transfer to San Francisco State University—where I also did not do well. Sir, I was also one of your first janitors here. Cleaning toilets came naturally, as I am from the Untouchable caste in India. I was also one of your first gardeners; many of the trees on campus that you see out this window were planted by me. I say to your students: Never give up, even when things look gloomy."

As baseball legend Babe Ruth said, "It's hard to beat a person who never gives up."

If, when I was a student at Skyline College, someone had said that I would be the Corporate Controller of the third-largest savings bank in the United States or a

Senior Vice President of Finance at Bank of America, I would never have believed it. Back then, if someone had said that I would go to Harvard or be a professor at UC Berkeley, I would have simply laughed it off. If someone had said that I would be invited by the world's richest man, Warren Buffett, to spend a day at his home in Omaha, I would have asked myself, "Who am I to deserve this?"

Back then, if someone had said that the President of India would one day call on me to seek advice, I would have been blown away. If someone had said that the Prime Minister of India would invite me to build frameworks for Smart Cities throughout the country, I would have said that it was just a dream. Back in my early days at Skyline, if someone had said that the Chief Minister of my state in India would commission me to return to my village to build better business models to improve people's lives, I would have never believed it. But it all happened.

As the American fashion designer, Tommy Hilfiger, said, "The road to success is not easy to navigate, but with hard work, drive, and passion, it's possible to achieve the American Dream."

I continued my speech. "Sir, I am here today to share with your students the truth that hard work always pays off." In 1984, in one of my earlier jobs after receiving my MBA, I was hired as a low-paid accountant at GlenFed Inc., the holding company of Glendale Federal Bank, the third largest savings bank in the country. I always worked late into the night in the basement in one of the company's many dreary buildings. The janitor and I were always the last to leave the premises, close to midnight. I worked on a report that one of the executives referred to Keith Russell, the President of the bank. My analysis showed how tighter policies on small expenditures would generate substantial savings for the division.

After reading the report, the president wanted to know who the author was—the man with the incredible name, "Solomon Darwin."

He was told that I was an immigrant, the dark Indian fellow working out of a basement in one of our more remote buildings. One day, I got a call from the President's secretary. I was nervous and thought that I was getting fired. I went down several streets to the "Ivory Tower" at 500 North Brand Boulevard, our corporate headquarters. Going through security gates was a new experience for me. I entered the bank presidents' lavishly furnished office on the fourteenth floor, overlooking the Glendale Hills.

A very tall man welcomed me and had me take a seat. I anxiously sat at the edge of it, not knowing what all this was about. He opened the report and said, "This is very impressive, and I need more strategic thinkers like you." This meeting changed my career trajectory for the rest of my life.

Keith Russell made arrangements to send me to the Harvard Business School. Even for the president of a leading bank, however, this was no easy thing. Harvard rejected me twice because I was too young and was not a member of the bank's senior management team. But Keith Russell did not give up, and kept petitioning until I got in. He had to write lengthy letters to Professor

William Brun, the director of the Management Development Program. Their concern was that I would not be able to bond with the senior executives representing the other global brands who were accepted into the program, such as the CFO of the Ford Motor Company and the Corporate Controller of Carnation, both of whom were assigned to my project group.

Upon completing the MCCP management program (an executive management program), I returned to Glenfed as the Corporate Controller of the bank and was given the corner office overlooking Los Angeles. This was a steep and incredible promotion that had bypassed many levels of management. I was the envy of many executives who had previously been far senior to me, many of whom also hated that "the dark Indian fellow" who had raced past them on the corporate ladder. I served in this position for several years until the bank was acquired by a larger firm.

I concluded my speech at Skyline by stating, "Sir, in this country, hard work will be recognized; I observed it and experienced it personally in my own life. I would encourage your students to work hard."

I was hardly the first to offer this advice. As Margaret Thatcher (who, as Britain's first female prime minister, also had experience doing things that were impossible based on the circumstances of one's birth) said "I do not know anyone who has gotten to the top without hard work. That is the recipe. It will not always get you to the top but should get you pretty near."

Naming Names

Despite my dismal academic performance at Skyline, I was accepted, somehow, as a transfer student at San Francisco State. My performance was still below average, though much better than it was at Skyline College. In addition to struggling with my classes, as the eldest son I had the obligation to support my father in putting food on the table for the family of seven. I took on a full-time job at a busy restaurant down the street as a janitor and dishwasher. One day the cook didn't show up; I filled in for him and continued to be a cook after that. I worked the graveyard shift from 11 p.m. to 7 a.m. while attending college during the day.

This restaurant I worked at was part of a chain called Sambo's. The décor of the restaurant was based on the story of "Little Black Sambo," who tricks some tigers into chasing each other at such great speed that they dissolve into a pool of butter. Sometimes at the restaurant, I was asked to put on a turban and dress up like the Sambo character, while another employee would dress like a tiger. This was even written up in the restaurant's corporate newsletter. While the Sambo character was sometimes applauded as a dark-skinned hero in children's stories, at the time it was generally viewed as an unhealthy stereotype.

Having known the entrenched discrimination of India's cast system, the irony of finding myself working a restaurant that many people viewed as perpetuating America's own version of a racial caste system was not lost on me. But human nature is similar throughout the world. At the time, I was very taken with the speeches of Martin Luther King, Jr.. I was fascinated by him and memorized his speeches. While I saw parallels with the challenges that both America and India faced with the baseness of human nature, the values on which American had been founded made me think America was better prepared to overcome them.

As a full-time student working a full-time job, my schoolwork was already suffering, as I couldn't keep up with the homework and other assignments. In addition, my father was pushing me to pursue a career as a doctor. I knew that that was simply not possible. I didn't have the grades or the competence to pass any kind of entrance test at any medical school. But he either didn't understand or didn't accept this. To make him happy, I enrolled as a pre-med student and began working toward a bachelor's degree in biology.

This put me on a course (or actually, in a course— a biology course) where I would have the opportunity to confront my own name.

At birth, my father had named me Charles Darwin. It was his hope that I would honor that name by following in Darwin's footsteps and finding definitive proof for his theory of evolution. As a child, that was the name I went by. But that wasn't the first name I'd had, nor was it the last one that I would have.

In India, Untouchable families have house names that reflect their status. An Untouchable who decides to embrace Christianity—and rejects the caste of their birth-- will often adopt a new name. Sometimes the new name is a Biblical one; sometimes it is a secular name that avoids proclaiming the stigma of being an Untouchable, but also avoids calling attention to their Christian beliefs. When my father was embracing Communism, for example, he adopted the name Soma Raju, which sidestepped both the Untouchable family name of Nalli, a type of bedbug (which was still required for legal purposes) and the Biblical name Solomon that Subbamma had given him.

When I was born, my dad was completing his PhD in biology and wanted me to pursue a career in science as well. He embraced the Communist view of the world that sought a more equitable life for all people and rejected the religious views that permeated Indian culture. My grandmother hoped that her grandson would become a missionary and help the less fortunate, in the way missionaries had helped her. She wanted me to be named for St. Paul to reflect her aspirations for me.

Even in my cradle, there were two names fighting to shape my destiny. Shortly after I was born, I actually had two names at the same time—or no names at all, depending on how you look at things. My grandmother had taken me back to the hospital where I was born to register my new name. When she arrived with me, however, I had fallen into a coma, and they said they couldn't admit a dead body. She stayed with me at the hospital all night, until I finally moved, and the hospital agreed to take me in. She hated the name Charles Darwin, so when they asked what name to register for the baby, she named me for St. Paul. I was a baby with two names. Before the coma, I had one name;

afterwards, I had another. And during the coma, I was presumed dead, with no name registered.

When I was born, the name my father wanted me to have—Charles Darwin—won that battle. But only for a while. When he later became a Christian, he changed my first name to Solomon to reflect his new direction, and the direction he hoped that I would take. Subbamma had prayed that if I was allowed to live, she would see that I was named Paul. Eventually, she made good on that promise in her own way by making sure that my brother, born right after me, was given that name.

These naming conventions may seem confusing, but in the Indian culture—and especially, among Untouchables—they communicate the purpose and destiny of a person. An Indian meeting another Indian will ask not what your name is, but what your house (or family) name is. If you meet an Indian with a Christian name, you can be virtually certain they are an Untouchable; nearly all Christians in India are Untouchables.

Evolving Viewpoints

My name has become a bit of a preoccupation for me. When people hear the name "Solomon Darwin," they sometimes think it must be nerve-wracking to have a name that traps Darwin together with a Biblical king. Sometimes my wife asks me: Which one are you, anyway? You have two distinct personalities in there. (She prefers the Solomon side over the Darwin side.)

As a young boy growing up, I still went by Charles. I wanted to learn more about the "other" Charles Darwin, so when I was admitted to San Francisco State University, I took a class in Human Evolution taught by Dr. Dean Kenyon, a prominent Stanford PhD. and an expert in the chemical origins of life. During the first class, as he was calling the roll, he came to my name and stopped. He looked around and could not find a grandiose-looking Englishman.

I had not raised my hand high enough for him to see me. I was sitting in the front row and raised my hand a little higher. He looked perplexed and said, "You are no relation to Charles Darwin, right?" "Right," I said. He paused again and said, "You will be a great inspiration to me in this class."

My curiosity about my namesake grew. I read all the books about the theory of evolution in my father's library; some argued for it, and some against it. Armed with this knowledge, I challenged Dean Kenyon every day in class. He seemed to grow frustrated and angry. One day, he asked me to visit him in his office. I went in fear of being dismissed from the class. He asked why I was taking his class. I told him of my father's desire for me to study medicine.

I also explained why I was named Charles Darwin, and how later my father changed it to Solomon Darwin when he started believing in God and abandoned the theory of evolution. I said that his class was about finding proof in dead fossils, but that I find living proof in people like my grandmother and mom, and their conviction that God is real. He seemed sincerely interested in my grandmother's story and kept encouraging me to share more. I continued until he broke down, saying that deep in his heart he had the same convictions. On that very day, he became a follower of Christ.

This happened on a Thursday and he visited my church that Sunday in nearby Pacifica to share his testimony from the pulpit. Pastor Ron Fields at the Little Brown Church had been counseling me about my struggle with the rational theory of evolution vs. my faith-based belief in the creation story. Like Dr. Kenyon, Pastor Fields had also been intrigued by my name. I had been his student in Sunday school when I first arrived from India and, two years earlier, he had given me a book that included Darwin's thoughts about his own faith. Pastor Fields had underlined a passage, and written comments in the margin advising me to not stray from God.

After several sessions with me, he said he didn't know which way I would turn. But he told me that he did know one thing: He said I was being led astray, and he wanted to break that professor's leg! When I told him the good news that Dr. Kenyon would be coming to church next Sunday, he was taken aback, as were the elders of my church. It was one of the proudest days of my life. My father was in the audience as Dr. Kenyon gave his testimony about his newfound faith in following Jesus.

Of course, this was very disturbing news for the university. He and I appeared on the news the following week, and Professor Kenyon would never teach evolution again at San Francisco State University. He shifted his focus in a different direction: developing, writing about, and promoting the notion of intelligent design. His book on "Biochemical Predestination" had special relevance to me. In the book, he asserts there can be no design without a designer. He argues that the chance of life spontaneously emerging on earth is a vanishingly small mathematical improbability. After careful study of the conflicting beliefs, I also came to believe that the intricate designs we see at the atomic, molecular, and biological levels require an Almighty Designer.

My academic performance continued to be poor, but I had discovered the purpose behind my curious name of Charles Darwin. I was privileged to be a catalyst that changed Dr. Kenyon's direction in life, and he went on to influence many others through his books and publications about his ideas on intelligent design. While I wound up getting a "C" in his class, he claims that I was the most purposeful and best student of his teaching career. We remain in touch to this day.

Discovering the Leader Within

I was an Untouchable living in a strange and foreign country, with very little education. I was often highly stressed, and frequently depressed. But in 1978, I discovered that I had surprisingly useful leadership and organizational skills. This self-discovery eventually led me to earn an MBA, which helped me ascend to senior positions at Motorola, Glenfed Bank, First Interstate Bank, and Bank of America.

This is how my discovery unfolded. Upon hearing the story of my life, the pastor of my church, Ron Fields, came to me and said that God has put it in his heart to go to Mori. He asked me if I could organize the trip. No one had ever asked me to take on such a big responsibility. I had just turned 23 and had never managed people, raised funds, or organized anything. Leadership had been laid upon my shoulders. However unequipped for the task I might have felt, I could not say no because I felt that I was called by God to do this.

I wasn't sure what Pastor Fields had in mind, but the vision I conceived for the trip was lofty and ambitious.

Our mission would be to care for people who were imprisoned in the remote village society that perpetuates poverty and the caste system. We would show compassion and love to them, just as Jesus had done in Israel. It was my nature to dream big like my grandmother. I said that if we were going to travel that far, let us conduct camps in several locations around Mori over a period of six weeks where thousands could attend each day. I proposed to organize a 100-voice choir that would travel with us every day to all these locations to inspire the crowd. We would work with all of the 30 local churches to attract crowds each day. I said to the pastor, "Let us make this a great expedition like that of David Livingstone's trip to Africa."

Mori village was (and still is) a remote place; it would take several airplanes, both international and domestic, to get us there. Once we arrived, we would need to take an overnight train and several rickshaws from the train station to the ferry. There, we would cross the Godavari River on primitive canoes while our luggage would follow behind us in oxcarts. The logistics would be far from simple.

This project also meant that I had to organize and execute many tasks: to recruit a competent team, create a budget, raise funds, establish networks both here in the U.S. and in India, and inspire 30 churches in and around Mori to participate. To my surprise, I was able to navigate my way through these activities, orchestrate them, and make it all happen. The event was a great success. I realized that God had equipped me with previously unknown administrative skills and a given me a driving passion to serve people.

While we were in Mori, Pastor Fields went up to the terrace of the sole concrete building in the village. I had gone ahead of the group a couple of months earlier to have that building constructed. Untouchables could only afford to live in mud huts, but our mission had raised enough money so that I could pay for the construction of more comfortable lodgings for our group.

The new concrete structure, with bathrooms along the side, was located just across the tile home where my grandparents, parents, and I grew up. Ron went upstairs to pray and to be alone. He saw a vision of the future, which he later shared with me, along with two other members of our party, Mr. and Mrs. Jack Boynton. (The Boyntons were active members of our church; he was a vice president at Wells Fargo, and she was a nurse.)

In Pastor Fields' vision, he saw a school in the rice fields that stretched out all the way to the main road. He saw that the cinema theater on the main road that kept us up all night had shut down and the building would become a part of the school facilities. He saw a hospital in the adjacent rice fields that would house the midwifery services that my grandmother had started. When I heard this, I said it was impossible because the rice fields were not part of the Untouchable village, that they were owned by landlords who would never sell them to someone from our caste.

On the way back from India, I said to Pastor Fields, "If I were to die today, I will have no regrets, as the capabilities granted to me by God were put to good use and I feel very satisfied about the outcomes of the expedition."

Ron passed away in a freak accident shortly after we returned. I gave no further thought to his vision and dismissed it—until much later.

Jack Boynton also disappeared from my life when he moved away to Bakersfield. It was twenty years later when I ran into Jack at a McDonald's while I was travelling from Los Angeles to San Francisco on

Highway 5. He came over to our table where my family was having lunch and asked if I was Solomon Darwin. I said "yes" and shared with him some great news: "Remember when we were in Mori, Ron had a vision on the terrace? It has all come true.

The landowner had a heart attack and needed money, and his family came to me hoping I could buy his land. It now houses the international school that Ron saw, educating 400 kids. The cinema theater was converted to a rice mill; when the owner of the mill went bankrupt, he sold it to the school. The adjoining land that belonged to the temple was auctioned off because the temple needed money; I bid for it, was able to buy it for very little, and we built a hospital there, just as Ron foresaw. Jack couldn't believe this. He and his wife visited Mori to witness the fulfillment of this extraordinary prediction that, at the time, seemed like a fantasy.

Before this mission to Mori, I had had no experience leading anything. I had no skills in things like fundraising, planning, building structures, or setting up institutions and operating them. When I look back at my life, I find the handiwork of Jesus at work—building, shaping, and equipping me for this kind of challenge. I also believe that Jesus brought significant people into my life to help me with ambitious projects like establishing a school and a hospital. Money for these projects was donated by people I had not met before. The sequence of events flowed seamlessly without force, like water flows from high to low. I have no other way to explain my destiny.

Finding My Calling

At the airport in Visakhapatnam, as I was leaving India with my father for good in 1971, I turned around to say goodbye to my grandparents thinking I might not see them again. It was an emotional time for me; I felt that I was cutting my umbilical cord from the paternal protection of my grandfather and maternal love of my grandmother. I held my grandfather's hand and looked up at him—he was 6'4"—and I whispered sadly, "Tha-

Tha, I am leaving." I have never known a nobler or more generous man. I did not know then that I would never see him again. I went over and embraced my grandmother who raised me like her own son and went through much grief with me.

We could not pull ourselves apart as they called me to board. As I ran, she came running after me and said, "When you return, come back as a missionary to serve people." Those words did not mean anything to me then, and I made no commitments, neither to her nor in my heart.

What I did not know then was that in 1988 I would return from America with her dead body, to bury her next to her husband. This is when the calling in my life became very clear. Only then did I realize the gravity of the request she had made. It was a missionary who saved her life, who taught her how to read and write, who helped her and her husband to make their living as merchants, and who provided her with access to global markets to conduct her lace business. It was the same missionary who prayed for her to be able to conceive the son she bore at age 38—my father, who would later take me to America.

My grandfather passed away in 1972 and in 1978, my grandmother came to the US to live with my parents, which she did until 1988. At one point, she came to bless my new home in Valencia, California. (I had just moved from a home in Long Beach.) At this time, I was happily settled in my corporate controller job at Glenfed. She came up to my corner office on the top floor of 500 North Brand and said that I was blessed—like Joseph, who managed the wealth of Egypt. After watching me conduct business for a while, I knew she was proud. With a look of amazement in her eyes, she said: "Be a good steward and a blessing to people."

Upon returning to my house, she developed allergies due to the fresh paint in my new home and she could not breathe. The next day, she was taken to Henry Mayo Newhall Hospital in Valencia where a young doctor accidentally punctured her lung while giving her an IV. Her lung collapsed, and she went into a coma. While she was passing in and out of coma for several weeks, she forgave her doctors and cautioned her grandson not to sue them for medical malpractice. She also asked me to take her body to India when she died. I said I could not fulfill this request, as I had just been promoted and was in the middle of planning a conference that would be an important opportunity to further my career.

She told some of her children standing by her bedside about a personal encounter with Jesus she had during one three-week stretch of her coma. She saw the Heavenly Realm—its mansions and people, including her parents, husband, and baby brothers who had become grown men in the Spiritual Realm. She said that no human language is capable of describing a place or state beyond time and space, where she had been cleansed by the blood of Jesus.

The final leg of her hospitalization was in Casa Grande Hospital in Arizona, close to her son, Dr. Elias Nalli. There, she would often wake up and complain about the Native Americans that kept bothering her all night. She had no knowledge that Casa Grande Hospital was built on an Indian burial ground. She wanted to return to her peaceful Eternal Home. Her connection to the Spiritual Realm continued to deepen, and she had prophetic visions in which Jesus revealed my son to her.

She called me in L.A. and asked me to come immediately, as her time was near. She had shared these visions of my son with my uncle and aunt. I was not married then, so when I arrived everyone assumed I had an illegitimate son somewhere. Now I realize that Jesus showed her my only son, Judah, who bears a resemblance to Subbamma's tall and fair-skinned husband.

I arrived that same day at 10 p.m. and found her struggling to breathe. As soon as she saw me, I saw a twinkle in her eye. She gathered her strength and grabbed my red tie and pulled my face down close to her and kissed me. We communicated with our eyes as she was now unable to speak. She was turning blue as the oxygen failed to enter her bloodstream, despite the many life-support machines attached to her, so I took my last chance to whisper in her ear that I would keep my promise and return her body to Mori to bury her next to her husband.

Shortly thereafter, she breathed her last and returned to her Eternal Home. I had gone to fetch my cousin; by the time we returned, she was gone. The machines had been removed from her body and an empty silence hung over the room. I could feel her absence. My dear grandmother Subbamma had passed away at the age of 98.

My secretary, Ann, observed that I was very depressed when I returned from the hospital. She learned what had happened and conveyed the news to other secretaries on the floor. Finally, the word reached the ears of Carmen, the President's secretary. Suddenly, I got a call from Keith Russell who said to me that I should not have any regrets about missing time at work; he would give me two weeks off to follow through on my grandmother's request.

I felt the hand of Jesus once again miraculously providing for me to fulfill her final wish when my first house in Long Beach was sold that very week; I would be able to fund the $15,000 needed to send her coffin back to Mori. I quickly made arrangements, had her mortal body embalmed and brought her to Mori, her final resting place on the earth where she had fought a good fight while serving people and upholding her faith in Jesus.

My journey back to Mori with her coffin did more than fulfill her request of me; it also changed the direction of my life. My calling became clear when the people who carried the coffin laid it in front of the mud-hut school that she had funded and that I, too, had attended. Her funeral was filled with people she had raised, named, nurtured, tended to. The impact she had had on her community was clear as day.

I returned to the U.S. to sell my home in Valencia, as I planned to go back to India to begin the work of replacing the hut with the international state-of-the-art school that is there today—a three-story building that can house 1,000 students. The University of Southern California donated a computer lab, and we were the first school in India to have a professional website and an email account.

Finding the One

After returning to America, my corporate controller position came to an abrupt end in 1992 when a new CFO was hired by the board to prepare the bank for an acquisition. At this time, the foundation was being laid for the international school in Mori, and there were many construction setbacks. My presence was needed to closely oversee construction of the school and to deal with the inevitable wrinkles and headaches. I had been unable to find anyone there who was capable of managing this task for the village, so I moved to India. After several months, I ran out of money. Most of my money went into laying the foundation and a few walls. I was being laughed at by many people, including my dad, who said "I told you so."

At this low point I realized the need for a helper who would be a "bone of my bones and flesh of my flesh," someone who would stand alongside me to help shoulder the burden that is sometimes too heavy for one person to bear. I started praying fervently, but I had to wait as the time had not yet come.

One day, as I was praying for help to relieve my financial and emotional bankruptcy, the phone rang. This phone, installed just the previous day, was the first one connecting the village to the rest of the world. The first call I received was from Paul Mullings, who had been my boss at Glenfed. He said that for months he had been looking for me for months and was happy to have found me in Mori. He had asked many people for their help in tracking me down. He was now the Chief Financial Officer at First Interstate Bank, and was offering me the position of Finance Director, at a hefty salary.

I took the next plane to Los Angeles and started my job that very week, in July of 1993. Given the construction crisis in the Mori project, I sent 90% of my paycheck to Mori to finish the construction of the school. I lived very frugally on the remaining $450 per month. I moved into the U.S. Center for the World Mission in Pasadena where I shared a room with four other guys. For $450, the center provided me shared housing and three meals a day. This was meant for poor missionaries who could not afford housing, not for well-off bankers like me. But my roommates understood my calling and my situation.

Having found an answer to my financial bankruptcy, I was hoping to also end my emotional bankruptcy. Each night, I took walks praying for a wife. I felt the time was right. One day, I visited a nearby church and saw a beautiful girl in the front row worshiping very seriously. I found her praying and consoling other people after the service. I thought, "Now there is a missionary!" and I started praying about her during my walks. Her name was Amy, and it became very clear to me that she was the one.

I made many attempts to take her out, finally convincing her to go for a nice dinner at the New Delhi Palace in Pasadena. Over dinner, I shared my grandmother's story with her. She was moved, and we saw each other many times after that even though she did not feel that we were right for one another.

Eventually, she returned to her hometown of Wenatchee, Washington. But my prayers did not stop.

Many months later, I got a call from her, asking for help with her anthropology class in which she was studying tribal people of India. I was overjoyed, and I helped her with all of my strength. The same week I was offered a senior executive position in San Francisco at Bank of America's corporate headquarters.

My talks with Amy became more frequent, and she expressed an interest in coming to California and staying with my parents in their downstairs apartment. At this time, Bank of America was in negotiations to be acquired by NationsBank and my job came to end. I didn't want to move to the new headquarters in Charlotte, North Carolina, so I resigned from my job. One evening when we were at the Gaylord India Restaurant in San Francisco, I knelt down and asked Amy to marry me.

We had a simple wedding and moved to Mori the following month. At this time, I was broke, as I had been sending all my money to India to finish the building the school. Amy married me when I was unemployed and had nothing in my bank account. Deep inside, I felt she had a missionary heart and my grandmother would have approved. My mother loved her from the moment she met her. My dad was equally impressed with Amy from the time she entered his home.

Amy and I were welcomed into the Mori village by the local musical band and were ushered into the home where Subbamma lived and where I was raised as a child. Although we had been officially welcomed, Amy was often treated as an outsider in the village. As a beautiful 26-year-old blue-eyed blonde, she was the talk of the village; the kids and women in the village came around just to be with her, and that attention could be uncomfortable.

Amy also had to adjust to the loss of many of the comforts of life she'd been accustomed to. There wasn't clean water to bathe in. There was a lack of privacy, as people would often simple barge into our home. There were rats, mosquitoes, snakes, wall lizards, and insects of all sorts. She also had to adapt to the extreme heat, with no fans and frequent power outages, limited drinking water, and food that was unfamiliar to her. Despite all this, she kept herself busy and soon took charge of the orphanage that Subbamma had started. As a professional ballet dancer, she put her artistic talents to work and taught the kids there to dance, which brought her much joy.

I regret neglecting my young bride, as I was caught up with construction of the school. The daily challenges of the construction logistics consumed me; at times they were too much for me to bear.

But Amy would soon face an even bigger challenge, when she became "barefoot and pregnant" with our first daughter. Over a period of several months, she grew weak from a lack of good nutrition. I took her to closest mission hospital. We arrived at the gate and stood in line with hundreds of pregnant ladies waiting to be examined by Dr. Irene Leeser, a doctor from the UK who had served there for almost 50 years. While standing in the heat, I felt that I would faint and collapse from the heat before Amy would, and I feared that Amy would not be able to endure the wait until it was her turn. Fortunately, somebody noticed the white lady way back at the end of the line who was not accustomed to the heat and humidity and escorted us directly to see the 78-year-old Dr. Leeser.

As fate would have it, she was the same doctor who delivered me at the hospital across the river same forty years ago. She was also the one who revived my dying body when Subbamma brought me back to that hospital as a three-year-old baby. I was so happy to meet her, finally, as I heard so much about her service and dedication to our community there.

Upon seeing Amy's anemic condition, she immediately attended to her and took us into her residence. She generously gave Amy several packages of imported food products (from her own kitchen inventory) that might restore Amy's health. For a moment, I thought that perhaps she would deliver my own baby, but she sadly informed me that she would be returning for good to the UK at the end of the month to UK. I vividly recall how moved I was gazing upon the faces of the two beautiful white women sitting in front of me; they were far apart in age and generations removed from each other, but they shared the common experience of taking a risk and leaving the comforts of home to live in India.

They came willingly and selflessly to care for people who were not their own and embraced a people that they didn't know and fell in love with people who were so different from them. I have no rational words to explain their zeal to serve people and their zest for caring for those in need. But I could clearly see that they were sisters of the same heart, serving the same Master and having the spirit of Jesus living inside them.

We returned home bankrupt; fortunately, the American government covered the costs for my new baby Nena's birth, and we stayed with my parents. Paul Bryant, my friend from U.S. Center for World Mission who had joined us shortly after our arrival in Mori, took charge after we left. He remained to get the school started. The following year, Randy Thompson from the

Woodcrest School system in Riverside, California, arrived in Mori to establish the school's curriculum.

Amy has been a great source of strength and a sensible advisor throughout my life, especially during the early years when we were founding the ministry together. She advised me to go into teaching, rather than seeking work at another financial corporation, which she didn't think was the right fit for me. Sure enough, I got a call one day from my former professor at Harvard, Ken Merchant, who had taken on a new job as the dean at University of Southern California's Leventhal School of Accounting. He offered me a teaching job with a handsome salary that I could not refuse.

Amy and I moved to Southern California. For the next nine years we raised our two children there, while also managing the school in India. Raising Nena has been a source of joy—as a newborn, she made me forget the struggles of my first teaching job at a demanding and competitive school. I always had a smile on my face while driving home to hold her. I looked forward to taking her to the park along with her little brother Judah who came into our life a bit later. Judah was also a bundle of joy and Nena was an all-around delight. And, of course, Amy was a great mother besides being a great wife—she took great care of them during my busy schedule and trips away from home.

Opportunity Becomes Destiny

I often found myself cast into roles and jobs for which I was not equipped, educated, or trained. But my hunger for knowledge enabled me to be a quick learner.

When I was suddenly made the corporate controller—essentially the chief accounting officer—of the third largest savings bank in country, despite having no background in financial accounting - I thought my world would fall apart. I had only had had three introductory accounting classes, but I had CPAs reporting to me at the three banks where I had worked. Following my banking career, at the request of the dean at USC's Leventhal School of Accounting, I was appointed to be Professor of Accounting, where I won seven awards for best teacher in the subject during my nine- year tenure. I was recruited by UC Berkeley's Haas School of Business to teach accounting to their MBAs.

I was later asked to develop new courses, as well as a new Master's program in Accounting. Fortunately, I had worked with the "Big Four" accounting firms, with government agencies including the AICPA, FASB and SEC, as well as with the deans of colleges within the University of California system, so I was hopeful that the degree program could be implemented with success. Getting a degree program approved is no ordinary task. Many said that I could not do it, but I made it happen within the shortest time possible. The fact that I did not have in-depth knowledge of accounting did not matter; what did matter was my ability to adapt to the changing environment.

When my teaching position in accounting at UC Berkeley came to an end after five years, I had to look for a new job. I ran into Professor Henry Chesbrough, the "father of open innovation," in a hallway at Berkeley. He taught courses on business models and innovation.

This was a subject that I had not heard about before. But soon afterwards, I not only started teaching the subject but also became the Executive Director for the Center for Corporate Innovation.

I teach courses on open innovation and business models to people around the world and consult with many companies and government entities. Accounting and innovation are, in many ways, polar opposites because each requires a different mindset. I discovered my own strength in adapting to different circumstances. Perhaps this was a strength I learned through the struggles of my Untouchable youth.

When I returned to America after burying my grandmother in Mori, I told my father that I would build a large international school there. He laughed and said that I could not do it, as it would require a lot of money, engineers, and contractors to build. Without telephones or roads, how could I even manage the logistics? He said that even if I built such a school, I would not be able to run it because it requires too many resources, teachers, and administrators to keep it running. Managing it long-distance would be difficult, especially while also maintaining a demanding full-time job in America.

But today, beautiful buildings on a 10-acre campus house over 600 children and close to 70 staff and faculty. I learned how to oversee construction of buildings in India, deal with bureaucracy, establish a school, hire and manage staff from afar, and raise funds while holding a demanding job. I attribute this in part to my own adaptability and flexibility, but also to my passion and commitment to Jesus's calling in my life.

I had hunger for knowledge which helped me adapt easily to changing landscapes, but this only got me so far. Knowledge is not wisdom and I needed wisdom. Knowledge tells me how to survive and what to do, but wisdom tells me when to do it. Wisdom is the right use of knowledge. Wisdom requires judgement and discernment. Judgement and discernment are based on the moral values one holds. I draw inspiration from my Christian role models who personified Jesus in their lives. Today, it is my personal relationship with Jesus that guides me in my discernment.

"I shall pass this way but once; any good that I can do or any kindness I can show to any human being; let me do it now. Let me not defer nor neglect it, for I shall not pass this way again."

attributed to William Penn

Throughout the separation of my parents during my father's devotion to Communism and his TB episodes, until I was seven years old, Subbamma raised me as her own son. She read to me daily from "The Pilgrim's Progress", through which I met Jesus and developed my life values as well as my work ethic. She always called me her third and favorite son, saying I could do anything. It came as no surprise when she left her final words—and final call to action—to me.

Though Subbamma raised me, I didn't always appreciate her. She had frequent asthma attacks when she lived with our family in the US, and the burden fell on me to take her to the hospital. As a young man trying to finish my education and working my part-time job, I remember lashing out at her on the way to the hospital. I said to myself, "Why does this burden have to fall on me?" and wished her dead.

She replied, saying, "You were the cause of my asthma. I was healthy all my life." She explained, "When you were a baby abandoned by your parents, I raised you. One day, you were sick with an advanced case of jaundice and went into a coma."

"I hurried you across the river in a canoe to the mission hospital where you were born. The doctor said that I had killed the baby and refused to admit you. I laid you in one of the stretchers in the veranda outside the hospital and refused to take you back."

"All night long in that cold night, I prayed," she said. "My prayer was a wish: *Lord, let this baby live and he will serve you all the days of his life.* I pleaded and pleaded and fell asleep on the cold concrete floor. I woke up the next morning with a terrible asthma that never left me since. However, I thank God with every breath I take when I have an attack because you lived."

"One of the nurses passing by that morning saw that you were moving and took me in to register you." I knew that I had been born at that hospital with the name Charles Darwin, the name my evolutionist (at the time) father gave me, but Subbamma wanted to name me after St. Paul so I would become a missionary serving Jesus. This was her chance. Subbamma said, "I asked the nurse to register you as Paul. I wanted you to grow up and serve Jesus all the days of your life."

She told me that there is a mission hospital in Narsapur across the river from Mori where I was registered with two names. She advised me, "Be true to God because Jesus saved you. Be a missionary."

I also remembered then that she had spoken the same words just as I boarded the plane on my first trip to America at the age of 16 to join my father. She pulled me back and said, "When you return, come back as a missionary." I returned with her coffin, and it was my turn to respond to Jesus's call to people, just as Subbamma had.

"If I can help somebody as I pass along,
If I can cheer somebody, with a word or song,
If I can show somebody how
they're travelling wrong, then my living shall not be in
vain.

If I can do my duty as a good man ought,
if I can bring back beauty to a world up wrought,
If I can spread love's message as the
Master taught, then my living shall not be in vain."

Alma Androzzo

Throughout my life, I have benefited from the guidance I've received from several mentors. Like many children, my parents—especially my grandmother—guided me through my life, serving as role models I could learn from, take direction from, and find inspiration in. As you've read, I've also had several teachers, pastors, and professional colleagues that have played that role as well.

Many years ago, I chose Jesus to be my Master, the guide who I follow, who is always present, and who not only helps me make the difficult decisions in life but also helps me celebrate the joys as well. Many of my own mentors—my father, my grandmother, Dean Kenyon, and others—also ultimately made this same decision.

You may have found someone—or something—to follow as your guide through life. I am always intrigued to hear about who or what guides the lives of other people, how they came to understand that relationship, and what impact it has had on their lives. This book has largely been my own effort to share my answers to those questions. If you would like to share your own answers, I encourage you to visit the companion website for this book at www.peacefulevolutionpublishing.com. I look forward to learning more about you.

"But one thing I do, forgetting those things which are behind and reaching forward to those things which are ahead."

St. Paul

GRATITUDE

I have found my Master to be not merely a guiding presence, but also a channel for what I can only describe as Divine intervention. Here are some examples of how that presence revealed itself to me throughout the process of building a ministry in Mori.

Subbamma delivered almost every baby in the village during her time there. I wanted to continue her work by starting a small clinic—a ministry that could provide medical facilities, an orphanage, and other services to the village in her memory that would serve the people in Mori.

I had no idea how to make this a fully functioning reality. I had started work on this ministry and had some people working on it while I was away, but the project was woefully short of funding. A Swiss doctor, Dr. André Mermoud, visited the project while I was teaching in France, and the ministry's general manager put him in touch with me. He said he would be in France soon, and wanted to meet me there. We met, although nothing happened until the following year when I returned to France.

We met again at a small McDonald's in Lausanne. I told him my grandmother's story. The whole time I was telling him the story, he was drawing something on a napkin. Upon completion of my story, he turned the napkin around and showed me a beautiful drawing of a hospital. He said, "Go, build it." He sent more and more money to build a magnificent structure far beyond any architectural project in the area. He later surprised me by shipping enough state-of-the-art equipment to furnish it and fill three storage rooms. I just wanted a small clinic.

He later converted the rice mill across the street (which had long been a thorn in my side) into a beautiful center to dine and house international guests. The school had been completed in 1997, set in peaceful surrounding—with one exception.

The ugly-looking rice mill was making our kids sick, triggering allergies from the rice husk it sent into the air. We prayed for the rice mill to be shut down, and our prayers were answered—partially—when the owner told us he was bankrupt and would sell the mill location to us for $25,000. That was welcome news—except we didn't have that kind of money.

One day, after I returned to USC, I heard a knock on my office door. It was an elderly lady who introduced herself as Becky Christjaener, an alumna of our college. She had heard about my school in India from my friend Garry Parker. I took her to lunch at Commons, our faculty club, to share more about the school in India. She asked me about my needs for the school. I told her we had everything we needed, except for maybe a swing set for the kids to play on in the yard. After she finished her sandwich, she gave me an envelope that had a $60,000 check in it. She told me to use it to build a park in her husband's name, who was a missionary to China.

I said, "This is too much for a park." She gave me permission to use it for whatever was needed if there was anything left over. And indeed, we did build a beautiful park—some have called it the "Disneyland of

India"—and had enough money to purchase the rice mill.

As our school began to grow, we didn't have enough room to accommodate all of the children that were in need of the services we could provide. Three students were sleeping in one bed. Mosquitoes were rampant. We had no fans or adequate furniture. Randy Thompson and I laid the foundation for a new hostel building, even though we didn't know how we could fund its construction.

We called all the kids together and asked them to pray and ask Jesus to provide for us. We did not own the adjacent land; we just asked for it, we did not know where the funds would come from; we just petitioned for them. We needed over a $120,000 to build and furnish such a building.

Randy Thompson and I returned the following year and the building was standing there upon the foundation stone that was laid a year before. This is how it happened.

When I returned to USC, I received a call from someone I had never met. He said, "My name is Mike Van Daele. I wanted to know if you would be a mentor to my daughter who just got accepted to USC." I said that I would be happy to help and gave him my office room number to pass on to his daughter. Before I put the phone down, he said that he had heard about my school in India and that he would like to make a donation in appreciation for helping his daughter.

I said that would be fine, gave him my address, and said he could mail it to me, assuming it would be a few hundred dollars at most. I mentioned that I was late for my class and that I should be going.

But he wanted to ask if perhaps he should the check by registered mail. I didn't understand his concern—until he mentioned that it would be for $120,000, the exact amount we needed to put up our new building. I had to sit down to process this incredible news.

He also said to let him know if we ran short of funds to finish the building; later he offered to furnish it. Mike and Linda Van Daele have been a blessing to the school ever since. They have funded two of our school vans, as well as major renovations.

The small mud-hut and dirt-floor school in the village that Subbamma once donated is now transformed into an international school with more than 500 students. Back then, it was the first school in India to have its own webpage and email account.

A tiny village that is found nowhere on the map of India is now home to a school that won many awards and produced many graduates who have become successful both in India and abroad. The ministry now includes a modern hospital facility that serves the community on a far greater scale than the one-room birthing center in her home.

Shortly after the school opened, a prominent landlord's family, whom my grandmother worked for running his cashew processing unit, invited me for dinner in his home.

He and his sons served me a big feast, serving me at their table, although they did not sit down with me. They said that they had utmost respect for my family.

The man said, "I grew up watching your grandmother's life. She was never allowed in our home.

When she came here to collect her wages, my father used to make her stand at the dung heap where the cattle were kept, far away, and my servant would drop coins in her left hand. Today, I am so happy to have her grandson at my table and send my grandchildren to be educated at your school."

What I took away from this reconciliation of sorts was that while there are many forces that seek to divide the world, whether on the basis of caste, creed, race, gender, or religion, there are also some powerful forces driving towards a more equitable society. Those forces are access to entrepreneurship, education, and opportunity for all.

I've shared three stories from three generations. There's a common thread woven through all of them. My grandmother's strength was her entrepreneurial flair. My father's education emancipated his future. In my case, the opportunities presented to me in the

United States would not have been available in my native country.

But as different as our stories and our strengths are, we share a common set of faith-based values that were instilled in all three of us. These values helped us to prevail over the tempests and storms that confronted us.

And looking beyond my family's stories, I often wonder why it is that so many people have flocked to the shores of America? My sense is that for many people, they have been rejected elsewhere and are seeking opportunities where they will be treated fairly and equitably rewarded. This country is founded on faith-based values to empower people, from the days of the founding fathers until today. Indeed, all of the Ivy League schools in this country were established as divinity schools to train ministers to serve people. This nation generates more Nobel laureates from people of other nationalities than their own homelands do. Many countries excel at creating talent, but American culture is unique liberating and empowering them.

I am grateful to this country for the opportunities it has provided to me and to my family. I am thankful for the Divine Intervention that has helped and guided my family across the generations.

I am grateful to Charles Whitehouse for rescuing Subbamma, to Dr. Isaacs for his leap of faith in hiring an Untouchable biologist, to President Nixon for allowing my father to stay in America and to bring his family here, to my namesakes Charles Darwin and King Solomon, and to a remarkable 19th century gentleman named Arthur Cotton who provided a model for compassionate entrepreneurship (I encourage you to read more about his story).

My journey was made light by three great mentors: Pastor Ron Fields, Dr. Garry Parker, and Randy Thompson, for their selfless contribution to the work in Mori and unconditional love for the people of India. They were men sent from God to guide me along the way.

I am indebted to my friends Matt Sanders and Marion and Russell Pyle, for being there for me when I was having rough times running the work in Mori. Special thanks to my adopted son David Maracine and adopted daughter Martha Nalli for their dedication to the work in India for many, many years.

Looking toward the future, I've always tried to do my best as a husband and father. I am grateful to my wife, Amy Rani Darwin, and the rest of my family for supporting my calling in life.

Since an early age, my daughter Nena Rachel Darwin and son Judah Nalli Darwin have been concerned about the problems and injustices that plague our world. Both gave talks at the United Nations in the spring of 2017 about their individual missions. Judah was just 17, and he spoke about what America can learn from a small village in India.

At 16, Nena established her own organization to rehabilitate women who had been trafficked. Judah gave up a year of college at UC Berkeley to volunteer with the Smart Village Movement and says that he wants to run for the office of President of the United States.

Jaelle Flora Rani Darwin, my youngest, has ambitions to entertain the world as a film actor (a dream I also had at her age, which is as yet unfulfilled). My desire is that my children will be a great blessing to the world, and I feel that Amy and I did our best in showing them how to follow that path.

Most of all, I am indebted to my grandmother, Subbamma, my father, Solomon Raju, and their spouses, for the extraordinary examples they set for me in triumphing over their birthright and for the opportunity to share their remarkable stories.

OTHER BOOKS BY THE AUTHOR:

"The Road to Mori: Smart Villages of Tomorrow"

"The Balance Sheet of the Earth": Available soon for preorder on Amazon

Made in the USA
Coppell, TX
02 January 2020

13982871R00088